The
Clarity
Papers

Ann Latham

The
Clarity
Papers

The Executive's Guide to Clear Thinking and Better, Faster Results

Ann Latham
Uncommon Clarity®

RED OAK HILL
PRESS

RED OAK HILL
PRESS

Red Oak Hill Press, January 2018

THE CLARITY PAPERS

Copyright © 2018 by Ann Latham

ISBN: 978-0-9824684-6-3
eISBN: 978-0-9824684-7-0

Acknowledgements

First, I would not be a successful consultant without the support of my coach and mentor Alan Weiss, the brilliant rock star of consulting. I never even would have had the guts to quit my job without Alan. Being a part of his global community of amazing consultants has also been a source of tremendous growth and inspiration for me. I am particularly grateful for two colleagues, Dr. Andy Bass of Bass Clusker Consulting in Birmingham, England and Roberta Matuson of Matuson Consulting in Boston who have enthusiastically provided me with encouragement, great ideas, and advice for more than a decade.

I am also grateful for all my clients. I appreciate their loyalty, their honesty, and, of course, their referrals! One of the great things about consulting is the learning. I never fail to learn from every client. It would take too much space to thank them all individually for everything they've taught me and every way they've supported me, but I'd like to single out a few. I want to thank Rod Sitterly, owner of Sitterly Movers in Greenfield, Massachusetts, for being my very first client! If he reads this, I hope he smiles at the news! I'd also like to thank Perry Walraven, CEO of PCI, Inc. in Philadelphia, for his on-going business, support, and mutually enlightening conversations about business and life. Last, but not least, I'd like to thank Ed Gerding, VP at Boeing in St. Louis, for believing in me and the value of clarity long before others at Boeing finally caught on. To all the rest of you, I give my heartfelt thanks as well!

While I wouldn't be a consultant without those mentioned above and many others, this book would not be a book without Debs Jenkins, my endlessly enthusiastic, decisive, and perceptive editor from Spain.

And I'd be neither a consultant, nor an author, without my husband Rick. His unwavering faith in my abilities, encouragement, patience, and selfless willingness to keep the house functioning, the meals coming, and the wine cellar stocked while I'm immersed in work or traveling have been of immeasurable value to me. I could never thank him enough.

Other Books by Ann Latham

Clear Thoughts – Pragmatic Gems of Better Business Thinking (volume 1)

Clear Thoughts Volume 2 – Pragmatic Gems of Better Business Thinking (volume 2)

Uncommon Meetings – 7 Quick Tips for Better Results in Half the Time

Dedicated to my parents from whom I undoubtedly inherited my clarity, but whose clarity I did not fully recognize or appreciate until their deaths.

Contents

Acknowledgements

Other Books by Ann Latham

Introduction..1

PART ONE: CLARITY OF PURPOSE

Clarity for Strategy...15

PART TWO: CLARITY OF PROCESS

Clarity for Decisions..44

Clarity for Planning...59

Clarity for Problem Solving..84

Clarity for Time Management...103

Clarity for Meetings..136

PART THREE: CLARITY OF ROLES

Clarity for Leadership..161

Clarity for Accountability..178

Clarity for Commitment..199

Clarity for Feedback..227

This Could Be Your Competitive Edge, Unless You Delay....248

About Ann Latham...257

Testimonials..259

Introduction

Most well-run organizations understand the importance of goals, clear roles and responsibilities, and alignment. They establish strategic priorities and annual goals. They develop job descriptions, policies, rules, and training programs. They create well-defined and documented production processes. They also establish well-defined management systems that control things like performance reviews, budgeting, approval processes, and projects. All told, these constitute a yeoman's effort to create the three dimensions of clarity needed for productive, effective, committed employees:

- Clear purpose,
- Clear roles, and
- Clear process.

The resulting structure and controls are essential for allowing growing and shifting numbers of people to work together effectively.

But there's a problem with this: *It doesn't help employees get through their average work day.*

Why employees still lack clarity of purpose

Those annual goals, even if individualized and broken down by quarter, don't help people establish goals for the next hour, the next conversation, the next email, or the next meeting. Those annual goals don't help people figure out what to do when their priority list has gotten so long that they have no priorities. Those annual goals don't help much when priorities shift or projects fail. No, these top-down efforts to create clarity simply do not create the clarity of purpose employees need to be efficient and effective on a weekly, daily, and hourly basis. Furthermore, they simply can't. It isn't possible to create clarity in the moment from the top down.

Why employees still lack clarity of roles

Job descriptions and employee handbooks don't create sufficient clarity of roles either. Job descriptions have limited value when you are in the trenches. Actual roles vary with each request, each relationship, and availability. While you might be willing to leave the details of a project to Dean because he's a detail guy, you know you would be crazy to ask the same of Paul, who is never to be trusted with methodical, detailed tasks. And when Sarah is suddenly shipped off to troubleshoot at a customer site, you have no choice but to fill the gap yourself or find a substitute. Top-down efforts to predefine roles may make management feel as if everything is under control, but they can't possibly create the clarity of roles that employees need to deal with daily reality.

Why employees still lack clarity of process

The same can be said about clarity of process. Clear processes create efficiencies. But efforts to establish well-defined processes are generally limited to two types of processes: production processes and management system processes. Those processes don't help employees get through meetings or make decisions. They don't help employees solve messy problems. As a matter of fact, unless your work is closely tied to the production line, you may not even think of your work in terms of processes. This is especially true of knowledge workers and managers. No, top-down efforts do not create the kind of clarity of process that makes for efficient, highly-productive employees. And it can't! Top-down controls leave huge gaps.

So, how can you create clarity for your team, your groups, your company?

You need to create shared and Uncommon Clarity®

In *Your Brain at Work*, David Rock explains how brains function and how that knowledge can help you improve the way you work. My advice for creating clarity fits perfectly and provides tangible tips that will not only make your brain work better but will also maximize the performance of the brains with whom you are collaborating. The prefrontal cortex, according to David Rock:

- is where much of the heavy lifting occurs in our brains,
- tires easily because it is the newest, evolutionarily speaking, and simply not energy efficient,
- can only focus on one thing at a time,
- must simultaneously select and retrieve relevant information, push away irrelevant information, and process whatever needs processing.

That's a big job for a seriously limited resource! So how does *Uncommon Clarity®*, and especially shared clarity, help? In *The Clarity Papers* I'm going to give you the tools you need to:

- zero in on one thing at a time,
- more easily differentiate the relevant information from the irrelevant,
- get all the brains in the room on the same page, zeroed in on the same topic,
- get all the brains talking the same language and using the same criteria to separate the relevant from the irrelevant,
- help each other keep those brains focused.

What employees need, for up to 90% of the day, is the ability to create clarity every moment of every hour. They need to be able to establish goals, roles, and processes that fit any situation and give them and their co-workers the kind of clarity that makes everyone productive and effective. And they need to be able to create that on their own, when they need it. Yet, when organizations want to improve results, where do they focus their attention?

3

- They make new goals.
- The tighten up job descriptions.
- They write new policies.
- They lay on the training.
- They create new management systems.

In other words, they do everything they can to establish greater clarity from the top down. They do nothing to improve the organization's ability to create clarity as it is needed. If you want to make significant gains in productivity, engagement, and profits, your employees need to be really good at creating clarity in the moment! No one can do it for them.

If you're new to my *Uncommon Clarity®* thinking then this book will provide you with an overview of the three dimensions critical to achieving better, faster results. It will help you gain critical clarity and help your employees develop clarity for themselves and in synch with each other. This power of clarity will deliver better results, faster through smarter decisions, greater productivity, heightened commitment, and an increased ability of all employees to contribute to the best of their ability.

The Power of Clarity

The Power of Clarity that galvanizes commitment and drives high performance is built on three dimensions.

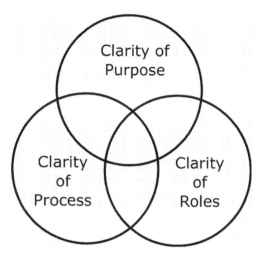

Clarity of Purpose

Clarity of purpose – knowing exactly *what* you are trying to accomplish and *why* – is critical to efficient, effective performance. Add focus to that equation and productivity soars.

If you want to maximize productivity, commitment, and results for the entire organization, you need clarity of purpose across the organization. You need strategic clarity – a compelling vision of what the organization needs to accomplish and why. You also need individual clarity – a universal ability to establish clarity so that everyone knows exactly what they need to do and why in each moment.

5

Strategy drives decisions at every level of an organization every single day. Or at least it should. Unfortunately, this isn't a given, nor is it actually very common. Too often, decisions are made based on myriad criteria irrelevant, or even counter-productive, to the organization's strategy. Criteria such as ease of implementation, conflict avoidance, local optimization, consistency for the sake of consistency, low hanging fruit, momentum, and personal passion.

To dramatically boost performance, an organization needs a clear strategy, employees who understand it enough to make smart and aligned decisions, employees who can create clarity in the moment to ensure their own productivity, and an environment that facilitates and permits focus.

When I first began consulting, I concentrated on operational excellence. However, it didn't take me long to realize that I couldn't help people execute more effectively if they didn't know what they were trying to accomplish. I've been helping organizations with their strategic thinking and planning ever since. For the same reason, Part One of this book will concentrate on strategy. I'll leave alignment for the sections on commitment and accountability, and focus for the section on time management

Clarity of Process

Once you and your employees know *what* you are trying to accomplish and *why*, you all need to know *how*. A good roadmap is invaluable for establishing clarity of process and can boost individual performance significantly.

Now if a process is understood by others, the benefits are even greater. If two of us have the same understanding and vocabulary to describe a process, we can help each other, correct each other, or step in and take over from one another. If you've already begun a process and I arrive late to the game, I can simply ask you what step you are on.

The value of shared process clarity is pretty obvious when you think in terms of processes that move physical objects. An assembly line. Order processing. Picking parts. But the value grows a thousand fold if you create shared process clarity for processes that move cognitive objects – processes that people don't even think of as processes. Processes like decision making.

Shared clarity of process for cognitive processes makes collaboration far more effective by focusing the collective brain power on a single clear step and making it easier for everyone to contribute effectively.

Imagine interjecting shared process clarity into every discussion and every meeting in your organization. You probably can't. Which is why you'll want to keep reading!

Clarity of Roles

The last dimension of clarity is knowing *who* is going to do what. Once again, the biggest opportunity lies in specificity, and the ability of employees to create in-the-moment clarity of roles.

But you can't just be *specific*, you need to be *explicit*. Too often we rely on assumptions instead of being explicit. "Joe hasn't complained, so this plan must be OK with purchasing." Never mind that Joe hasn't been paying any attention because he has been too busy planning his next vacation or worrying about a sick child.

Even diligent, attentive employees will sit up straighter if you point your finger at them and assign a responsibility. "I am counting on you to represent the front line supervisors, you to represent the customer's concerns, and your technical expertise to keep us out of trouble." Simply telling people specifically why you need them replaces lackadaisical passivity with an enhanced sense of purpose.

Explicit specificity has an additional benefit: it allows for negotiation. It provides an opportunity for people to suggest better representatives or to correct your assumptions about their expertise.

These three simple, easy to understand dimensions are all you need to take advantage of the power of clarity. Creating a *Culture of Clarity* isn't quite as easy. It requires a shift in thinking, new skills, practice, sharing, and, most powerful of all, speaking what I've coined as the *Language of Outcomes*.

Want Results? Speak the Language of Outcomes!

The tangible outcomes of progress are easy to measure: sales, profits, market penetration, and yield, as well as number of products, parts, members, programs, etc. Many employees are pretty clear about company goals in relation to these types of results. But only those on the production line can really tie their own productivity to these metrics: parts per hour, sales per week, hours per production, etc.

Everyone else spends a lot of time talking, thinking, writing, and reading, often with little to show for it. As a matter of fact, the farther they are from the assembly line, the more time spent this way and the less time spent producing tangible value for which customers are willing to pay. Are talking, thinking, writing, and reading important? Of course. Are they efficient? Rarely! Why? Because these people would be hard-pressed to declare significant clarity of purpose, process, and roles. If you want evidence, look no further than the conversations themselves. Simply put, few people are speaking and thinking in the *Language of Outcomes*.

The Dangers of Treadmill Verbs™

Look around you. Listen in on conversations. Read pretty much any meeting agenda. What will you find? Lots of people discussing, reporting, communicating, and reviewing – activities described by what I call *Treadmill Verbs*™.

8

Why do I call them that? Because you can discuss, report, communicate, and review *forever*! You can also update, share, respond, and explain *forever*! There is no way to know when you are finished. It's like running on a treadmill. You can always run a little farther. You can always talk a little longer. Here are just some of the many *Treadmill Verbs*™ that invite endless talking:

- Discuss.
- Report.
- Communicate.
- Review.
- Update.
- Explain.
- Respond.
- Write.
- Share.
- Describe.
- Teach.
- Coach.

Without a destination there is no way to know when you have arrived.

The Value of Destination Verbs

Destination Verbs, on the other hand, demand an outcome:

- Decide.
- Resolve.
- Plan.
- List.
- Confirm.
- Approve.
- Ask.
- Answer.

Destination Verbs drive outcomes because it is easy to know when you are done. You've either made a decision or you haven't. You've either approved, listed, answered, resolved, or confirmed, or you haven't. The state of being done is easily recognized and you can move on. You've made discernible progress.

Once you eliminate *Treadmill Verbs*™ from your vocabulary, you will be flying from destination to destination. Meanwhile, those speaking in *Treadmill Verbs*™ will still be reviewing, updating, and communicating with little clear idea of what it means to be done.

In Pursuit of Latham's Six Outcomes

To simplify the situation further, here are *Latham's Six Outcomes*. These six are the only outcomes that add up to real progress:

1. A decision.
2. A plan.
3. A problem resolution.
4. A list needed as input to one of the above.
5. Confirmation.
6. Authorization.

That's about it! *Decisions*, *plans*, and *problem resolutions* create progress. Tangible, measurable, discernible progress.

When you've made a decision, you are done. It's obvious. When you have a plan in hand, you are done. When you've resolved a problem, you are done. These aren't treadmills. These are tangible milestones.

Progress is also discernible if you *list* important inputs needed for any of the first three of *Latham's Six Outcomes*. For example, establishing a *list* of objectives to guide a decision represents tangible progress. Making a *list* of resources or assignments can be vital input for a plan. Identifying a *list* of possible causes is essential for problem solving. In all of these examples, when you've made your *list*, you are done! That's clear progress!

Note: If you aren't clear about the lists needed as inputs to decision making, planning, and problem solving, stay tuned. *Part Two: Clarity Of Process* will answer those questions.

Back to *Latham's Six Outcomes*. Sometimes the desired outcome needs to be nothing more than confirmation. This is the fifth of *Latham's Six Outcomes*. Seeking confirmation goes something like this: "This is what I am trying to accomplish, this is what I've done so far, and this is what I'm going to do next. Am I on the right track?" The only valid response to a query such as this is:

- Yes.
- No.
- Would you like to talk about ... (one of the aspects of your decision, plan, or problem resolution)?

Notice that the third response invokes another Yes or No and not an immediate discussion. Think about all the times a lack of clarity has transformed a simple request for confirmation into a lengthy unplanned and unnecessary discussion where someone fills your ear with information you already have or, on the flip side, aren't ready to receive. Has this happened to you?

11

The sixth of *Latham's Six Outcomes* is "May we proceed?" Authorization is just as straight-forward as Confirmation. It also should produce one of three responses:

- Yes.
- No.
- I need to understand more about your ... (decision, plan, or problem resolution).

If you want results, you need to speak the *Language of Outcomes*. You can't discuss, communicate, review, and report. Decide what decisions, plans, and problem resolutions you need and ask for them! Decide if you need confirmation or authorization and ask for it! If you aren't working towards one of *Latham's Six Outcomes*, where are you going?

Eliminate *Treadmill Verbs*™ from your vocabulary. Replace them with *Destination Verbs*. Ensure that every conversation, email, or document moves you one step closer to one of *Latham's Six Outcomes*. Get off the treadmill and start speaking the *Language of Outcomes!* With this first step your journey to clarity begins and, along with it, dramatically improved productivity, performance, and profits.

The Clarity Papers is a series of standalone, thematically related papers, organized so you can quickly find answers to your questions. I understand you are busy, so each paper will take just a few minutes to read and will provide you with plenty of tips, advice, and actionable ideas so you can gain clear thinking and better, faster results. Many of these articles have been previously published online and in places such as Forbes.com, where I am a regular contributor. As you read through the tools and techniques covered in the three dimensions – Purpose, Process and Roles – think about the *Language of Outcomes*. There is simply no substitute for knowing what you are trying to accomplish. That's strategic clarity and clarity generates better, faster results.

PART ONE:
CLARITY OF PURPOSE

"Too often, leaders tell employees what to do, but not why."
Ann Latham

Why You Need Greater Clarity of Purpose

What must be different when we are done?

The difference between effort and progress is measured in tangible results. Something you can point to or hold in your hand that wasn't there before. A new product or parts to build the product. A decision or a list of criteria to govern the decision. An observable and reliable new behavior. All of these constitute tangible progress. Something that is verifiably different.

Effort, activity, and busyness don't count. Talking about that product, going around and around on that decision, and planning to change behaviors is often just talk. With no discernible progress. Sometimes something more concrete emerges. But sometimes the talk and deciding and planning just go on and on.

To find the shortest and fastest path to progress, you should always be working toward a specific tangible result that moves you closer to your goal. This is true whether your focus is a year, month, week, day, or even the next quarter of an hour. It is true whether you are working in a group or sitting alone at your desk. You will accomplish far more far faster if you always know with great specificity what must be different when you are done.

No matter what you call these tangible steps toward progress – goals, objectives, initiatives, milestones, desired outcomes, action items, to-do list entries, or one of *Latham's Six Outcomes* – they create clarity of purpose. The more specific, the better. Without them, you wander. With them, you can focus, pick the right path, and know when you are done.

Since clarity of purpose begins with strategy and the top down decisions that should drive every other decision, I'll focus the rest of Part One there.

Clarity for Strategy

"When you invest your time and money in organizational improvements,
are you supporting a clear strategy or just improving operations?"
Ann Latham

Your strategy is the boss that ought to drive decisions at every level of your organization. Thus, you need to get crystal clear about the basics. How can you best create value, for whom, that you can deliver profitably, and in a way that sets you apart from your competition? You need a strong, realistic, focused game plan.

What the Heck is Strategy Anyway?

The biggest problem with the way organizations think about strategy is they confuse strategy with plans. They aren't the same thing. Strategic planning is an oxymoron. It is also the reason why strategic planning often misses the mark and why I always work extra closely with prospective clients to clarify expectations before I even agree to work with them.

Let's start with a definition.

A strategy is a framework for making decisions about how you will play the game of business. These decisions, which occur daily throughout the organization, include everything from capital investments to operational priorities to marketing to hiring to sales approaches to branding efforts to how each individual shuffles his To-Do list every single morning. Without a strategic framework to guide these decisions, the organization will run in too many different directions, accomplish little, squander profits, and suffer enormous confusion and discord.

15

Clarity of Purpose

What value will you create?

A strategic framework must establish what the organization will do to deliver value for which customers are willing to pay and how it expects to hit target revenues and profits. The strategy doesn't answer all the questions required for implementation – that's planning, but it clearly establishes the game you are playing and how you expect to win. It also identifies the games you aren't playing – the things you have no intention of delivering, even if your best customer begs you.

Identifying products, services, and target markets is only the beginning. The strategic framework must also establish the business model used to profitably create sufficient volumes of value.

What do you need to be really good at?

What core capabilities are essential to your success? This question affects everything from whether your salespeople need to be big personalities or technical gurus to whether your operations team needs to be adept at custom projects or high volume production. Clarifying which systems need to be top notch keeps everyone on the same page and investing in the right resources.

What sales and distribution channels will you use?

How will you reach customers? For example, will you hire salespeople, use sales reps, build stores, or sell through Amazon? Will you give keynotes to demonstrate your expertise as I do, or will you concentrate on SEO (search engine optimization) so customers find you on the Internet?

How will you deliver the goods? Electronically, by FedEx, with your own fleet of installation experts, with drones, or some other way?

These questions are essential to understanding necessary investments, establishing profit expectations, and determining what you need to be really good at.

What kind of revenue and profits should you expect?

What will it take to be profitable? What will it take to achieve expected sales volumes?

Why do you think you can beat the competition?

Businesses don't operate in a vacuum. When you play the game of business, you aren't the only kid in the sandbox. So your strategy also has to establish how you intend to win the game. What will make you stand out? Why will customers choose you over the guy down the block offering similar products and services? What is your competitive edge? Is it still valid? Drink too much company Kool-Aid and you'll forget that yesterday's edge is today's norm and tomorrow's joke.

Strategic clarity is the boss.

These are the big decisions that drive everything else — all your investments, hiring, development, timelines, etc. These are the big decisions that allow everyone to make cohesive plans and truly work toward the same objectives.

When I work with clients, few are ready to or need to start with a clean slate. The answers to the previous questions often seem completely obvious to them. And that's one of the reasons they need me or someone like me capable of shifting paradigms and challenging assumptions. All of these questions need to be on the table. If not, you will be incapable of making a dramatic change or taking advantage of big opportunities. Instead, you will simply plod along making incremental changes at best.

The Importance Of Strategic Focus

A good strategic framework provides focus by limiting the number of directions the organization runs and also controlling the speed. You'd be foolish to try to extend all your products while simultaneously expanding all your markets while also ramping up capacity or shifting your business model to include new types of production, sourcing, sales, delivery, and partnerships. This isn't just an issue of capacity. It is also an issue of risk, learning, complexity, and credibility.

For example, offering an existing product to an adjacent market (A) would involve relatively little risk and complexity and require limited learning. Credibility would likely be the biggest obstacle. Contrast that with offering a new product to a new market (B). In that case, you are embarking on significant risk, complexity, and learning with zero credibility. This grid provides an easy way to demonstrate the scope, magnitude, and synergy of the initiatives you are considering.

Creating Strategic Focus

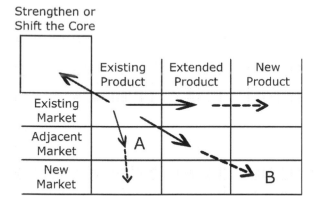

While working with a recent client, I had the senior team list all their current initiatives – full-bore, half-baked, and under serious consideration – on individual post-it notes. We then stuck them on a big grid like the one here. The visual impact was immediate. And, I might add, totally typical! They were trying to shift their core capabilities from custom products to high volume standardized products while also developing completely new products and trying to get into completely new markets. No wonder they were struggling!

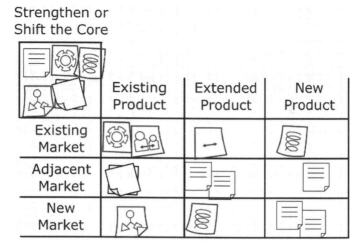

Create synergy and minimize complexity by moving horizontally into new products OR vertically into new markets OR straight up to strengthen or shift the core. Diagonal moves and multiple directions will leave you spread thin and unable to make the best use of your resources or existing capabilities.

Nothing beats strategic clarity and focus! Get clear about the value you will provide to whom, how you intend to win customers while also delivering profitably, and how to sequence your efforts to maximize synergy while minimizing chaos, complexity, and risk.

Strategy, Results, and Distractions – Beware Low-Hanging Fruit!

Is your organization quick to pick the low-hanging fruit? Do you gravitate first to the quick and easy? Are you prone to delay the bigger projects until you get those little ones out of the way?

Low-hanging fruit is, by definition, quick and easy to implement, thus the lure to pick it is compelling. And picking the first piece usually exposes another, leading to an infinite quantity of low-hanging temptations. While some of these quick fixes make excellent investments, many do not, and the nearly infinite supply can become a black hole for your limited resources.

Not only are the quick and easily-visualized fixes compelling, but the more important, strategic opportunities are often exactly the opposite because they can involve fundamental changes in how things are done. The most important initiatives will create an organization with new capabilities, new capacity, and new potential. These often require disruption to people, processes, resources, policies and/or technology. The complexity and level of departure from the norm can make both the goal and the path hard to visualize. The need for analysis and tough decisions ensures that many important opportunities will never be mistaken for low hanging fruit.

Here are some examples of low-hanging temptations:

"Let's get this system working right first."

- Improving the ease, speed or accuracy of data entry for data that is unused or ineffective in improving results.
- Increasing cycle count accuracy for inventory that should be disposed of.

"First, let me catch up on my email."

- Reading, sorting and responding to email that does not contribute to the goals of the company.

"I just need to get organized."

- Reorganizing files, electronic or paper, that are rarely, if ever, used.
- Updating schedules and plans that are mostly fiction.

"I know I can buy these parts for less somewhere else."

- Finding a cheaper supplier for a part that may be unneeded with strategic product positioning.

"While we are at it..."

- Adding that extra software feature while making needed changes.
- Fixing format inconsistencies in records before archiving them.

One glance at the diagram accentuates the dangers of pursuing low hanging fruit. You can readily see that success likely depends on a combination of easy and difficult tasks. You can also see that if your efforts are driven first by ease of implementation, you will squander resources on low hanging, unimportant fruit.

Clarity of Purpose

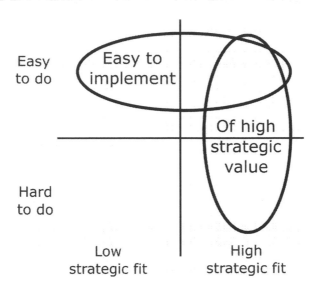

Easy to do

Easy to implement

Hard to do

Of high strategic value

Low strategic fit

High strategic fit

Are your resource decisions driven by low-hanging temptations?

You can't avoid inappropriate low-hanging temptations unless your employees are clear about the strategic objectives. Employees make decisions all day long that consume resources. If they do not know and understand the organization's direction and priorities, they will pursue low-hanging fruit. The only way to find out whether they are clear is for management to ask and listen.

Beyond that, you can listen for comments indicative of quick fixes, "We need to get a few things fixed and out of the way before we can start a bigger project." Strategic initiatives are rarely described as "getting things out of the way."

If you want to avoid the temptation of low-hanging fruit, the following are critical:

- Have a clear strategy – A clear strategy, well-communicated, with realistic expectations and only a few top priorities for any one individual makes it easier for everyone to focus on the right things.
- Assess each idea for strategic fit – Insist that alternatives are weighed against strategic goals first. Ease must come second. There is nothing wrong with choosing an easy path as long as the strategic benefits are strong. Resist the temptation to invest in easy initiatives of medium strategic value over harder initiatives of high strategic value.
- Remain vigilant – It is so tempting to tackle the quick and easy but 'tiny' tasks multiplied by infinity is a mighty big number!

Without strong vision, strategy and discipline, the low-hanging fruit will keep you busy for a long, long time, leaving strategic issues to languish. Accelerate progress toward your vision by pursuing the strategic over the easy.

How Often Should You Do Strategic Planning?

The Calendar Does Not Know Best

Many organizations adhere religiously to a strategic planning calendar. If they haven't done it in X years, it must be time! But what does the calendar know about the plight of your business? One year? Three years? Five? These are completely arbitrary time periods. How can an arbitrary time period, regardless of length, ensure that you are revisiting your game plan at the right time? Obviously, it can't! Don't rely on the calendar!

Clarity of Purpose

You Must Look Beyond Lunch

Some organizations wait until their competitors are about to eat their lunch before doing strategic planning. Obviously, this is another flawed trigger, and for three reasons. First, you will undoubtedly be too late. Playing catch-up or dodge ball is never a sound strategy. Second, if your competitors are mediocre, you will be mediocre too. Don't let your competitors determine how high you set your bar. Third, if you are gazing backwards at your competition, you will trip and fall on your face. Don't pay so much attention to your competitors that you fail to understand everything else that is happening around you, much of which is far more important.

Success Masks Failure

Some companies leap to action only when performance falls off the cliff or projections miss their mark in a big way. Bad numbers tell them it is time for strategic planning. This is also a big mistake.

When performance expectations are entirely disappointing, obviously you need to act. You need to figure out what's happening and why you are so far off track. You need to find the cause of your problem and make corrections. This might involve strategic changes. You may be playing the wrong game. But the cause could also be operational. Remember those three new sales guys you hired? Maybe they are selling too little and only your least profitable products. Don't blindly dive into strategic planning when the numbers are bad. Figure out what is going well and what isn't.

However, the biggest reason you shouldn't rely on bad numbers to trigger strategic planning is that sometimes you meet or exceed your goals. But that doesn't necessarily mean your strategy is a success. You could be succeeding in spite of your strategy.

Suppose your fabulous sales can be attributed to product A in China while you were expecting product B to take off in the Pacific Northwest. The China success is a wonderful surprise, but if that success masks your failed expectations for product B and prevents you from re-examining your strategy, that is really bad news. If you blindly celebrate your success without understanding why you are succeeding, you will continue pouring resources into product B and wasting precious resources and time. Don't let success mask failure! Avoid the temptation to ignore your strategy when you are successful. "Who cares? We had the best year ever!" is grounds for more strategic planning, not less, especially if you succeeded for unexpected reasons.

So When Should You Do Strategic Planning?

Every strategy is based on assumptions. These assumptions involve trends, market needs, demographics, government policy, the strength of the economy, competitor actions, technological developments, and much more. And these assumptions drive your decisions about what products you offer to whom, at what price, and with what profit. Most companies talk about these factors and agree on assumptions when establishing strategy, but many forget about those assumptions too quickly once the strategy is set.

It is those assumptions that you need to monitor, not just sales and profits. The minute one of your key assumptions proves false, your strategy is suspect. This could be as soon as the day after you finalize your strategic planning. Obvious examples of dashed assumptions include a crashing economy or a new law that makes your product illegal. Other assumptions are less obvious. In the previous example, the assumption that product B would appeal to Baby Boomers in the Pacific Northwest is an important assumption. Even if product B sells well in the Pacific Northwest, its purchase by new grads instead of Baby Boomers should be cause for concern because it proves a key assumption false.

Industry-wide indicators are less obvious. You may be assuming that the demand for air travel will continue to rise and you may think your sold out flights offer proof. However, if overall air travel is dropping, your current success is masking your failed assumption.

Keep track of the assumptions that form the foundation of your strategy and monitor the strength of each. If your confidence in those assumptions is starting to erode, it is time to revisit your strategy.

5 Signs Of Strategic Clarity And 10 Signs It's Missing

When I founded *Uncommon Clarity®*, Inc. over a decade ago, my initial focus was on creating organizational clarity so organizations could be more efficient and effective. However, it wasn't long before I discovered how little strategic clarity existed in most organizations. It is impossible to improve performance without strategic clarity. You have to know what you are trying to achieve before you can do it better! Trying to improve performance without strategic clarity is like trying to win a race without knowing which direction to run. If you cross the finish line first, it is either sheer luck or evidence of zero competition.

So how do you know if you are operating with strategic clarity? Here are five signs:

1. You know specifically where growth is expected in the next twelve months – which products, sectors, and geographic regions.
2. You know what drives your customers' buying decisions and have sharpened your competitive edge accordingly.
3. You know where to invest to support these priorities.
4. Your employees understand the priorities sufficiently to plan and achieve the prerequisites for success in time.
5. Daily decisions throughout the organization about what to do, what not to do, how well to do things, whom to hire, and whom to fire are clearly aligned with the strategic priorities.

If you tell me all five are true, I won't believe you if you also suffer from any of the following symptoms:

1. Your organization routinely struggles to hit important targets.
2. Your employees complain about too many priorities and poor communication.
3. You and your employees spend far too little time on activities for which customers are willing to pay. The vast majority of time is spent being exceedingly busy, but not productive. Customers are not eager to pay for time spent on unproductive meetings, email, chasing information, second guessing, reporting, analysis paralysis, rework, unnecessary approvals, and escalation of issues that should have been dealt with immediately by employees on the spot.
4. Improvement initiatives are driven by forces such as low-hanging fruit, HR, consistency for the sake of consistency, local optimization, and squeaky wheels, not by strategic priorities.
5. Products are 'gold-plated' with features that damage profits without increasing sales.
6. Under-performers manage to stay year after year.
7. Your employees can point to critical investments and changes that were discussed but never made.
8. Silos, egos, politics, blame, and excuses are frequent visitors at discussions of accountabilities.
9. Neither you, nor your employees, are able to take vacations, spend time with family, and take time for professional development.
10. Few seem to know how to say 'no.'

I've been called in to help companies of all sizes with each of these symptoms. More often than not, a lack of strategic clarity is a primary root cause for all ten of these problems.

9 Reasons Your Strategy Never Really Delivers As Hoped

Strategies fail more often than they succeed. Occasionally, it's because they are stupid strategies. Most of the times the cause is a lack of clarity – a lack of specificity about where you are headed, how you will get there, and what must change. Consider these examples of typical failures:

1. The leader can't really see the difference between the new vision and the previous trajectory

When I lead board and staff members in strategic planning, I shift their thinking about their organization and their options. You can see the ah-ha moment on their faces when the power of a new vision and strategy becomes clear. Unfortunately, the CEO is sometimes the one person who fails to experience that ah-ha. It could be defensiveness or maybe he has convinced himself that phenomenal success has been just around the corner for so long now that any new idea is simply an extension of his current trajectory. Maybe it is a little of each. Either way, if you can't see clearly how your new strategy differs from your current path, you are destined for incremental improvement at best. You will never become a significantly different organization capable of far greater accomplishments.

2. Insufficient buy-in from the staff and board

One of the first questions I like to ask staff and board before working with them to develop a new strategy is to tell me about their current strategy and priorities. Their comments are incredibly important and revealing, though they often tell a sad tale. This is where I find out how little agreement there has been about direction and priorities. It is also where I find out who was never on board after the last round of strategic planning. A strategy can't succeed if your critical players believe it is doomed to fail or that their ideas are better. You need clear buy-in. You must uncover and resolve those doubts, concerns, and disagreements.

3. Too many priorities

My strategic planning surveys also reveal insufficient focus with epidemic frequency. A good strategy creates a clear focus. You know you've achieved that clarity when employees have the confidence to set things aside and say 'no' to everything from customer orders to the boss' orders. A clear strategy tells employees what they should *stop* doing in addition to what they should start or continue doing.

4. Inadequate attention to the outside world

When you are eager to deliver on your commitments, keep your customers happy, and improve your operations, it can be difficult to think strategically beyond the status quo and operational necessities, and to really direct sufficient attention to the external world and trends affecting you and your customers. This is especially true if you think of your company as locally focused, not particularly dependent upon technology, or unaffected by Amazon and other significant disrupters. To be successful, you absolutely need to entertain fundamental questions about your value, markets, channels, visibility, and business model.

5. Inability to get above the daily grind

The daily grind can be a powerful inhibitor of strategic thinking. When the pressure and fear are almost overwhelming, strategic planning participants, especially those who are less strategic to start with, tend to respond to almost every idea with "yes, but..." They simply can't envision possibilities without also seeing crippling constraints: shrunken budgets, deferred maintenance, and staffing shortages, to name a few. A critical distinction that I often have to make is to separate strategy from implementation. Once you are clear about the difference and realize that most of the constraints that strangle your best thinking are related to implementation, it becomes easier to set these aside in order to see bigger possibilities.

29

Clarity of Purpose

6. Decision makers who aren't strategic

Occasionally, I encounter a strategic planning group comprised of zero strategic thinkers. They are cautious, concrete, linear, and officious. These are the people who are more concerned about defining stringent screening criteria and processes for selecting a consultant than in the ability of the consultant to shake them up and get results. They rarely produce a clear or compelling strategy. A far more likely outcome is more of the same with shiny new labels and a lot of pomp and circumstance. A client told me recently that they selected me out of several obviously capable consultants because I seemed the one most likely to make them uncomfortable. That's the sign of a group ready to see differently, think strategically, and seriously consider significant change.

7. Operational issues take precedence

Too often I encounter organizations with a 'strategy' that is nothing more than a program of operational improvements. The senior team convenes for annual 'strategic planning' and then plans for internal improvements without ever thinking strategically. These organizations need to learn the difference between strategy and planning. They survive thanks to luck. When the luck fails, so do they.

8. Implementation is the hardest part

Strategies don't just happen. You don't penetrate new markets or enhance production capabilities with wishful thinking. Every strategy must be translated into responsibilities and a series of actions with the involvement of those people responsible for implementation. Authority and resources must accompany those responsibilities and qualified individuals must assume those responsibilities. I've seen too many leaders essentially toss the strategic decree over the wall, cover their eyes and ears, and grit their teeth while they hope the magic happens. Of course I've seen the flip side as well: the leaders who try to orchestrate everything from the top because they don't trust their people or don't have people to trust and lack the courage to fix that problem.

9. Failing to build an organization capable of delivering

Many organizations are simply incapable of delivering on a new strategy. This is especially true if that strategy is at all ambitious. The CEO may not be strong enough to step up to a new game. The sales team may not be able to embrace a new value proposition. The operations manager may have been fine running a sleepy shop, but might not have a clue how to deliver precision results at high volumes. Any number of employees may not be ready for significant changes in technology. Production facilities may require dramatic overhauling. Leaders who fail to rectify the short-comings of their current capabilities will fail to implement their strategy. I've seen this happen time and again, especially when key players, including CEOs, aren't replaced promptly.

Strategies succeed when strategic thinkers establish a clear, focused, and compelling picture of how they will play the game of business. Leaders need to know, with specificity, where they are headed, what kind of organization they need to become, and how they will get there. Specificity is key. Without specificity, you'll just have a lot of interesting conversations and no alignment behind real change.

10 Ways To Stand Out From The Crowd And Win In The Game Of Business

Just because you build it doesn't mean they will come. You need to give customers clear reasons to part with their money and to do so with you. The clearer you are about what constitutes your competitive advantage, the easier it is to focus your efforts and investments, market your products, and convince your customers. Don't fall into the trap of believing all anyone cares about is the price. Here are 10 perfectly good reasons why your products and services could be chosen over those of other companies.

1. Price

Price is frequently a strong component of the customer's buying decision. This is Walmart's *raison d'être*. But price isn't the only consideration. And sometimes it is one of the least important factors. It is a huge mistake to think customers aren't willing to pay more for the other factors on this list. However, if you plan to win on the basis of price, you better have a really low price!

2. Quality

Think about the times when quality matters to you. A recent purchase just doesn't cut it and you are determined to find something that does. You are buying a gift for a special person and want to be sure it's of excellent quality. You need something you can rely on. There are innumerable situations when excellent performance and quality beats price. You could be buying a TV, selecting a moving company, or hiring a consultant. 'You get what you pay for' is a common expression, even though a higher price is no guarantee of quality. However, if you plan to win on the basis of quality--and have customers that return--your products and services better provide the quality your customers are expecting!

3. Speed

Sometimes speed matters almost more than anything. When your water heater starts leaking or your garage door won't open or even when you just can't wait to get the latest volume by your favorite author, speed matters. People are clearly willing to pay for speed.

However, speed is relative. In some cases, such as the burst water heater, speed means same day if not sooner. In other cases, such as a new custom home, speed means faster than average for that type of house. Just keep in mind that 'faster than average' keeps changing, especially in this age of next day delivery. Do you remember the days when you waited for the quarterly Sears and Roebuck catalog, begged your parents to write a check, mailed your order, and were happy to receive those brand new sand colored jeans at least a month later? My, have times changed! If you plan to win on the basis of speed, understand current expectations and figure out how you can shorten the path to results for your customers.

4. Risk

Reduced risk is compelling in many situations and well worth the money. Sometimes less risk is simply a benefit of buying great quality, and if the superior quality of your products and services is your competitive edge, you can often advertise risk reduction as part of your value. But sometimes reducing risk is entirely separate from quality. Examples include insurance, on-call service contracts, and warranties, as well as less tangible advantages such as knowledge or close relationships that convince customers you have their back and will go above and beyond to ensure their success. If you plan to win by reducing risk, you must understand the risks your customers face, figure out how you can reduce those risks, and deliver unerringly.

33

5. Convenience/Ease

I love doing business with people who make it easy for me. Easy answers, easy ordering, and just an easy experience from the first contact to the last. Amazon makes it incredibly easy by putting practically everything imaginable on their website, delivering within two days, and answering phone calls with competence, no questions, and better than expected solutions. But easy need not be so comprehensive. Think about all of the times companies leave you on hold, force you to create online accounts and change passwords, make you call back, and leave you unsatisfied. The bar is pretty low here. To make convenience and ease your competitive edge, you need to examine your customers' experience from top to bottom and make doing business with you a welcome breeze.

6. Lifestyle

I use lifestyle to explain many purchases that just don't make sense under any other category. It's always someone else's lifestyle I'm talking about, of course! I'll probably offend some of you by listing a few examples, but tattoos, ripped jeans, and giant luxury hotel suites come to mind. Of course, it also includes many things of which I partake: travel, sports, and electric cars. People will definitely pay for their style and pleasure.

7. Integration

Apple wins the integration game in my life. How could I possibly switch to another brand when my iPhone, iPad, iMac, and MacBook Air all work together so well? Integration is a way to insinuate your products and services into the very fabric of daily operations for both companies and individuals. If you want to win by integrating, you need to create a family of products and services that are independent but also create more value through interdependence. Imagine a clothing store that saw to it my individual purchases always matched things I already owned and always created fabulous outfits! I could be hooked for life!

8. Ultra coolness

Apple also wins in the supercool category. That's why everyone is lining up to buy the next iPhone. While they may be the kings of ultra-coolness, there are plenty of gadgets touted on Facebook as super cool. Just this week I learned about an appliance that replaces six other appliances, comes with a backpack, and gets your kids to school on time! Well, almost.

9. Prestige

While you may be eager to flaunt your supercool products and your lifestyle products, you might also just revel in their awesomeness at home alone. Prestige products are another story. Half, maybe all, of the point is to impress others. A Bentley, Jaguar, and Lamborghini fit the bill. Of course, if you live in the right place, a couple of these are good lifestyle options too.

10. Loyalty

Loyalty is another powerful edge. Typical approaches include a decent product, convenience/ease, and member benefits. Dunkin Donuts has made me a loyal customer using exactly that method. First off, I like their coffee. Secondly, they are ubiquitous in the areas I frequent and I don't have to add my own cream! That last one might seem silly unless you see how often I run out of other coffee shops only to return because I forgot to add my own half and half! Third, their app earns me free beverages and makes it easy to pay without cash and without feeling guilty about using a credit card for a little purchase.

But loyalty can also be built through very close relationships. If you have a decent product and a reasonable price, you can tip the scales by building the kind of relationship that keeps customers coming back. It is hard for a customer to walk away from someone who has repeatedly gone out of their way to meet their needs. Perhaps they could save a buck or gain a new feature elsewhere, but will a new vendor be there for them? Why risk it!

Clarity of Purpose

What's your competitive edge?

Play with the chart to help you establish your competitive edge. Before you begin, here are some definitions.

- Lagging = Falling short of customer expectations.
- Competitive = Meeting or slightly exceeding expectations.
- Out front = Clearly ahead of the game.

Place an N in the proper column of each row to represent where you stand Now. Use C1, C2, etc., to rate your main Competitors. Use F to mark where you would like to be in the Future. Feel free to modify or add rows to paint a better picture of your customers' priorities.

	Lagging	Competitive	Out Front
Price			
Quality			
Speed			
Risk			
Convenience/Ease			
Lifestyle			
Integration			
Ultra coolness			
Prestige			
Loyalty			

You can't be Out Front in every category, so choose wisely based on your target market, and focus your attention and resources accordingly. Also, think hard about settling for Lagging in any category because that can lead to customer dissatisfaction pretty quickly.

Clear Distinctions: Strategy vs. Plans

Strategic planning is an oxymoron. Throwing these two words around together constantly has done a lot of damage. When I help clients with 'strategic planning,' I have to undo a lot of that harm. The distinction between strategy and planning is critical, especially if your goal is to create a compelling and successful future.

When you develop a strategy, you need to be looking at:

- Market wants and needs,
- Products and services you could offer to address those wants and needs,
- Business models that allow you to reach target markets and fill those needs profitably,
- Opportunities to differentiate yourself from the competition,
- Your passions and values.

Assuming you have been successful in the past, your best ideas will come from examining changes around you. Changes in technology, demographics, market needs, the economy, etc., But also things you've learned, especially your worst failures, greatest successes, and biggest surprises of both kinds. The key to developing a strong and winning strategy is to think big, look outside the company, get out of your current mindset, stop thinking about limitations, forget about the 'how,' and paint possibilities that are out there a ways.

Planning is the exact opposite. It is rooted in the present, all about the 'how,' the gaps, your weaknesses, and logical next steps. It's an entirely different mindset.

Clarity of Purpose

Without a clear distinction between strategy and planning, the planning mentality usually dominates and the results are usually incremental at best. Instead of envisioning possibilities, people envision implementation difficulties. This totally colors and limits their thinking. SWOT, the ever popular strategic planning tool that itemizes strengths, weaknesses, opportunities, and threats, feeds this planning mentality at the expense of strategic thought. Half of the four SWOT quadrants are admittedly internally focused. The other two are usually anchored in that mindset – 'opportunities accessible from here' with no guarantee that market needs and the other strategic factors will be raised. This is not the road to new thinking and a compelling strategy.

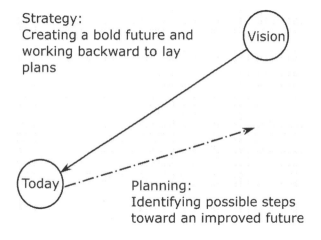

Strategy:
Creating a bold future and
working backward to lay
plans

Vision

Today

Planning:
Identifying possible steps
toward an improved future

The graphic provides a visual summary of the important distinction between strategy and planning. With the former, you think big, envision a new future, and then work backwards to make it a reality. When planning, you move forward one step at a time from the status quo. A strong strategy can put you on the moon. Planning will get you across town. We look at Planning in the next dimension, Clarity of Process.

Clarity Quiz – How Often Should You Do Strategic Planning?

How often should you do strategic planning?

1. Every year.
2. Every 3 to 5 years.
3. Whenever you suspect the competition is about to eat your lunch.
4. Whenever sales and profits fall significantly short of goals.
5. None of the above.

If you chose #5, congratulations! If you chose anything else, go back and read *How Often Should You Do Strategic Planning* earlier in this section. Simply stated, it is time to do strategic planning as soon as the assumptions underlying your current strategy prove to be false.

In Conclusion – What Does a Clear and Compelling Strategy Look Like?

A clear and compelling strategy:

- Is focused, competitive, and profitable.
- Builds unique capabilities to provide distinctive value.
- Leads to smart, aligned daily decisions throughout the organization.
- Leaves you feeling confident about the future of your company.

A clear and compelling strategy is not:

- A plan, especially not a thick one that collects dust.
- An event, like your annual physical, to endure and check off the list.
- A mom-and-apple-pie statement on a plastic card.
- Set in stone.
- Worth anything unless it is implemented.

PART TWO:
CLARITY OF PROCESS

"Disengagement is the result of frustrated efforts to be productive and creative in an environment that hinders both."

Ann Latham

Why You Need Greater Clarity of Process

When my parents died, their wills suggested an onerous process for dividing belongings among five siblings. But at least they provided a process! They also indicated we were welcome to come up with a better process, if we so desired. My parents, who probably had something to do with my clarity(!), clearly knew the importance of having a process!

As executrix, I gladly proposed a better process. Being me, I'm pretty sure I would have done so regardless of whether or not it was my responsibility. So I wrote up a simple process, explained it to all siblings, asked for opinions, and then got their signatures to confirm agreement before anyone began claiming anything.

The process worked smoothly. Success depended only on each sibling investing reasonable thought in their desires and needs. Everyone left with a combination of cherished and practical items.

There was one opportunity for dissension, however. I was the only one who had indicated a desire for the contents of the wine cellar! By the rules of the process, that made it mine. I let them howl for a minute, and then capitulated and agreed to take only a one fifth share. The alternative may have led to revolt!

So other than one completely predictable and anticipated glitch for which I was prepared, a clear process prevented all kinds of potential problems.

The Value of Process Clarity

Whenever you want to accomplish almost anything that involves other people, it pays to have a process. The benefits are many:

- Reduces conflict.
- Allows everyone to participate to the best of their ability regardless of personal characteristics such as rank, position, experience, age, or gender.

Clarity of Process

- Minimizes duplication of effort as well as dropped balls.
- Frees people to disengage where they neither care nor believe they can contribute.
- Increases commitment to any decisions or other outcomes of the process.
- Produces better results a lot faster.

Following a clear process is like playing a game. Those who know the rules can either play or sit out. Those who don't, can ask for an explanation and then play, observe, pair up with another player, or opt out altogether. The level of involvement and investment is at each individual's discretion. It doesn't matter whether the game involves the distribution of an inheritance or the purchase of items ranging from a candy bar to a home or making a meeting productive. When everyone knows how to play the game, they are more likely to do it well and support the outcomes.

Operating without such clarity leaves people guessing as to their roles and next steps. They don't know whether to invent and negotiate the rules, observe quietly in an effort to learn, or just charge ahead in pursuit of their own objectives. They can't maximize the value of their time and energy. When there is no process, nothing is predictable. And despite their best efforts, they won't necessarily respect either the process or the outcome.

I think the value of process is probably pretty obvious. What I think few people realize is how often they operate without the benefits of a helpful process when one would be incredibly valuable.

How often do you have to guess about direction and next steps? How often do you find yourself jockeying for position or trying to direct the action so you can contribute effectively and so the outcomes are sound? How often are you sitting in meetings with no discernible process? How often are you involved in decisions where a process would save hours and hours while also producing better results?

Pay attention during your next few days at work. When are you following a useful process and when aren't you? What's the ratio? 50-50? 30-70? 10-90? A clear process leads to better, faster results.

Clarity for Decisions

"If you can't agree on the destination,
you will never agree on the route."
Ann Latham

SOAR Through Decisions™ by executing all four steps of decision making in order. You don't want to skip the 1st, 2nd, and 4th like most people do!

Top Decision-Making Mistakes

If I had to pick the top two mistakes when making decisions, they would be jumping to alternatives and investing more time than a decision is worth.

Decision Mistake #1: Jumping to alternatives

When a decision is needed, people tend to immediately discuss alternatives or latch on to a particular alternative, "Let's buy a Prius!" Unfortunately, this is step three of the four steps of decision making. Resist this temptation and you will save numerous hours and avoid going down a potentially unfortunate path.

Decision Mistake #2: Letting investment exceed value

The investment of time, money, and energy in any decision must be in proportion to its potential to improve results or reduce risk. The top pitfalls include:

- Over analysis (though not necessarily accompanied by a disciplined decision process).
- Over involvement of people for all the wrong reasons.
- Making a big deal of an unimportant issue.

So to avoid these decision-making mistakes and get to that decision faster, read on.

SOAR Through Decisions™ – How to Make Better Decisions Faster

People can work together most effectively when they share an understanding of a process they are using, where they are in that process, and what comes next. This holds true whether you are helping a youngster tie a shoe or helping your company prepare the annual budget. I call this shared process clarity.

Unfortunately, one of the most common and consequential processes people use is also the most abused: decision making.

If your reaction to that statement is, "Process?" my point is made. Every decision requires four basic steps[1]. Unfortunately, most people muddle all steps into one messy, often prolonged, conversation. That's like making the 'bunny ear' loops before doing the 'first part of a bow.' When it comes to decision making, shared process clarity is extremely rare.

The good news is that the decision-making process is pretty simple, universal, and rewarding! Once you have a shared understanding of distinct steps of decision making:

- Decisions will be faster and better.
- There will be less stress and frustration.
- Employees at any level will be able to participate more easily.
- Commitment will increase.
- Whiners, dominators, and generally 'difficult people' will become far less conspicuous and troublesome.
- You will involve fewer people overall and more of the right people at the right time.
- Delegation will be easier for both managers and employees.
- You will save tremendous time.

---

[1] Objectives, Alternatives, and Risks come from a Kepner-Tregoe course I took once, and is covered in their book: *The New Rational Manager.*

There are only four steps needed to make a sound decision. The problem is, the natural tendency seems to be to skip three of them. To make better decisions faster, *SOAR Through Decisions™*.

SOAR™ Through Decisions (The Present)

- Statement
- Objectives
- Alternatives
- Risks

1. S is for Statement

State the decision that needs to be made. Sounds ridiculously simple, I know, but I guarantee you will be amazed at how often you and your colleagues are not actually making the same decision!

For example, suppose you mention to a group of friends or colleagues that you are thinking about getting a new car. Their reactions flood the room:

- Get a hybrid.
- Get a Tesla.
- Which car are you replacing?
- Do you plan to buy or lease?
- What will you use it for?
- Your wife will want a minivan.

These are pretty typical reactions and I'm sure you could add to the list. Take a look at the full list. How many different decisions are actually represented here? I count eight. Any conversation that conflates eight distinct decisions is inefficient.

The same type of *Disclarity* muddles numerous business decisions every day. Consider a discussion about a new product launch. In your head the question is which product idea to launch first. Meanwhile, your colleagues are questioning whether to launch anything this year, how to launch a specific product, how soon to launch, with what objective, and under what conditions. While all of those decisions may need to be made, being explicit creates the clarity that puts everyone on the same page and makes the right decisions in the right order. This simple step will save your company thousands of hours every month, if not every week or day.

Stating the decision is easier to do if you recognize that every decision is just one decision in a series of cascading decisions. You need to figure out where you are in that cascade:

- What decisions have already been made?
- Which decision are we making now?
- What decisions need to be made next?

Recognizing the cascading series and making the current decision explicit is particularly important when working with others. However, that recognition is also valuable when working alone. You might be surprised by how hard it can be and at how much time you save by creating that clarity instead of bouncing around in your own head among multiple related decisions. The S in SOAR™ stands for *state the specific decision at hand*. What a simple way to create critical clarity!

Clarity of Process

2. O is for Objectives

Determine the objectives. These are the decision criteria that must govern the decision and will allow you to assess the quality of your options. They include priorities as well limitations such as budgets, resources, and time. Some are just 'wishes' and some are 'musts.' And their relative importance matters.

When you hear people going around and around trying to nail down pros and cons or advocating for a favorite idea, it's because they haven't agreed on objectives. If you can't agree on objectives, you will never agree on an alternative.

Consciously treating this as a distinct step will save even more time than Step 1, and that's saying a lot! Furthermore, it will also improve relationships and bolster commitment because a good conversation about objectives, priorities, and limitations allows everyone to get their concerns on the table and find common ground.

How will you know a good decision when you see one? You must have answers to these questions to recognize the best alternative:

- What are you trying to accomplish?
- What are the decision criteria – objectives, priorities, and limitations – that should govern this decision?
- Which are absolute, black and white 'musts' that will be used to eliminate some of the alternatives?
- Which 'wants' are most and least important?

When working with a group, know that you will never agree on an alternative if you can't agree on objectives.

Let's return to the example of the car purchase. Suppose the decision is to select a car that will be used primarily for commuting alone over a considerable distance. The important criteria are likely to include mileage, price, safety, driver comfort, and sound system. Less important criteria may be the number of doors, factory installed navigation, the color, and whether the car is new or used.

The objectives can, and often should, be ranked in order of importance so that you can be sure the choice you make satisfies the most important objectives. In addition to ranking objectives, you should separate your 'musts' from your 'wants.' A 'must' represents a go/no-go criteria. In the case of the car purchase, a 'must' might be that the price does not exceed your budget. You would be foolish to sacrifice a 'must' like your budget in favor of a 'want' such as a particular sound system. You shouldn't even be looking at cars that fail to pass a go/no-go test such as budget.

Don't make the common mistake of skipping this step. Clarify your objectives before continuing to the third step of decision making.

3. A is for Alternatives

Alternatives are the possibilities you select amongst as you make your decision. This step is never skipped, but that doesn't mean it can't be improved. The biggest mistake comes from considering too few possibilities. The first ideas that come to mind are generally driven by recency, pet peeves, personal favorites, and old habits. Crash through those barriers by brainstorming lots of ideas quickly and without judgment. Don't rely on the same old gang. Tap some fresh eyes. Be creative. There are always more alternatives than you first realize. Those first possibilities that pop into mind are rarely the best!

Include the status quo on your list of alternatives. Even if you have no intention of staying the course, the status quo is a great reference point because you know it best and can use it as a comparison.

Clarity of Process

Strive for more ideas. After the first handful of possibilities is identified, there is usually a lull. Don't assume that means you've uncovered all the best options. The lull usually means you've only gotten through the most obvious ideas.

Once you've generated a great list, decide which alternatives best meet the objectives established in Step 2. Once you've *SOAR*ed a few times, you'll be delighted to see how quickly this process can go and how rarely personalities, baggage, and politics enter into the equation.

Be careful here; we are not finished. An exciting alternative often causes people to grab it and run, skipping the fourth important step of decision making.

4. R is for Risks

Once you have identified one or more top alternatives, you must consider the risks involved with each. Make a list. Can you live with those risks? If not, figure out a way to reduce the risk, or toss out that alternative and move on to another. Many bad choices could have been avoided simply by pausing long enough to ask yourself a few questions:

- What could go wrong?
- How likely is such a problem?
- How serious would it be should the problem occur?
- If serious or likely or both, what can we do to prevent or minimize its likelihood?
- What can we do to minimize impact should the problem occur despite our best efforts to prevent it?
- Can we live with the risk?

Despite a great process through steps 1, 2 and 3, this final step can easily lead to nixing an exciting idea. And that is why skipping this step is so dangerous. The world is full of examples where no one took the time to consider unintended consequences but ran with an exciting idea instead. Netflix comes to mind. They suffered a massive departure of subscribers and a stock plunge of 35% when they split their streaming and DVD service and raised prices. Somehow I doubt they answered these questions.

For example, suppose your favorite alternative when choosing a car is a new model with a new type of engine, lots of new technology, no track record for quality, no track record for delivering on time, and a dearth of fueling/recharging stations in much of the country. Other than that, it is simply *awesome*. Is that enough to give you cold feet?

Don't skip steps and suffer the consequences. Statement, Objectives, Alternatives, Risks. SOAR™ in that order. Every time you make a decision. Start practicing today. You will be surprised at how much more easily and quickly you arrive at noticeably better and more comfortable decisions.

We make thousands of decisions every day. Whether big or little, important or trivial, unilateral or group efforts, decision making can be really hard, painful, time-consuming, and ineffective. To create shared process clarity for decisions, you must *SOAR Through decisions*™!

Whom Should I Invite To My Decision?

Whom should you invite to your decision? I'm glad you asked!

Most people invite the same old group to all their decisions. The whole department, the same old management team, the entire marketing team, etc. Standing meetings with default attendees too often determine who is 'invited.'

Clarity of Process

The result is wasted time by those with little to contribute, poor decisions if the group is uninformed or ill-equipped to make the decision, and anger from those who thought they should have been included.

In order to invite wisely, there are two main considerations: making a good decision and ensuring the decision is accepted.

Ensuring the quality of your decision

To ensure a good decision, you need people with the right knowledge, expertise, and authority. If you look at the four steps of decision making separately, selecting the right people becomes much simpler. Furthermore, you will realize that you may need different people for different steps in the process:

Whose input do you need to establish the objectives and decision criteria?

They need to be able to answer questions like:

- What are we trying to accomplish?
- What are the most important considerations or priorities that should govern this decision?
- What limitations must be kept in mind (timing, budget, scope, interdependencies)?

You can't make a good decision without answers to these questions. And while many people may be able to make valuable contributions to this discussion, the ultimate authority for establishing the final decision criteria may lie with an executive, not a broad group. Good input and clear expectations and roles are important if you are to establish solid, reliable objectives and decision criteria.

Whose input do you need to identify and evaluate alternatives?

There are almost always more alternatives than meets the eye. A little creativity by those with the right expertise can work wonders in coming up with new approaches. If you invite the same old group, you are less likely to hear fresh ideas.

Furthermore, it should be pretty obvious that in many circumstances, the people setting the objectives and decisions criteria are not the best ones to generate or evaluate alternatives. If this isn't obvious, picture a large technical decision. While upper management may have to set or approve the objectives and main decision criteria, they aren't in a position to propose alternatives. Even for smaller, non-technical decisions this is often true. Brainstorming and evaluating alternatives often requires very different expertise from establishing objectives.

Whose input do you need to evaluate risks?

Evaluating the risks of the preferred alternatives may require different expertise from generating alternatives. And actually, you may need different people to evaluate the risks of each of the preferred alternatives! For example, suppose you are deciding how to deal with too little parking space and your preferred alternatives come down to allowing more people to work at home or building a parking ramp. Identifying and mitigating the risks of these two cases demand entirely different types of expertise! Don't let the same old management team try to identify and mitigate these risks!

Ensuring acceptance of your decision

To ensure acceptance of your decision, you need to involve the people whose commitment and actions are needed to support your efforts. In general, this means anyone affected. This is especially true of those from whom you need new behaviors.

Clarity of Process

People care most about decisions that affect their work and themselves personally. While they might prefer every decision clearly goes their way, they generally accept decisions that they believe were decided using a decision process that is fair and informed. Even bad decisions are readily accepted, and actively defended, when people believe the process was fair and informed. On the flip side, good decisions can cause riots when the process is perceived as unfair. Thus, if you want acceptance, strive for a fair and informed process:

- Follow the decision-making steps described in SOAR™.
- Let people know where you are in the process and who is or will be involved in each step.
- Be open to suggestions as to who should participate to ensure those most affected by the decision believe that their interests are represented.
- Keep in mind that different steps and different situations require different participants. In the previous example, getting buy-in for working at home vs. building a parking ramp likely involves totally different groups.
- Be transparent about the outcomes of each of the three steps.

Since an informed decision is part and parcel of ensuring a quality decision, the 'extra' time and effort required to ensure acceptance, need not be extensive. However, the broader and greater the impact of a decision, the more care you must take. Regardless of the magnitude of the decision, you can make substantial changes with good speed and minimal discord if you follow these simple guidelines.

How To Get Unstuck When Making Decisions

Too often I encounter leaders and employees struggling to make decisions. This is especially common with group decisions. Typically, the group is considering two or three alternatives with lists of pros and cons for each. They go around and around and just can't seem to reach a conclusion. So here is my advice.

1. SOAR Through Decisions™ with a disciplined process.

Follow my *SOAR Through Decisions*™ process. If you haven't been SOARing, you will probably have to move backwards to move forward. Most likely you are stuck on Step #3 because you short-changed Step #2, and maybe even Step #1. A disciplined decision process is especially valuable for group decisions. Even groups of two. It gets everyone on the same page.

2. Consider the importance of the decision.

Some decisions just aren't very important. They don't deserve a lot of your precious time. They certainly aren't worth a lot of stress. It always pays to assess the importance of a decision before you get embroiled in it. Don't even let yourself begin to agonize over an unimportant decision. Pick an alternative and move on to Step #4 – Risks. What is the down side? If you can live with the downside or minimize it, then be done and move on. Not every decision has to be perfect. This is especially true for unimportant decisions.

3. Examine the actual gap between alternatives.

If you are still stuck, compare the alternatives. Are they really that different? Will they really produce different results in the long run? I can't tell you how often I meet people weighing options endlessly when the consequences look virtually identical. Pick the easiest path or flip a coin and move on.

4. Reframe the decision.

If you are wrestling with an important decision, SOARing with discipline, considering a variety of alternatives, and still stuck, you may be trying to make the wrong decision. Go back to Step #1 of SOAR™ and reconsider the decision at hand. What are you trying to accomplish? If you are debating A vs. B or Yes vs. No, I guarantee that you are making the wrong decision. Step up a level. A decision such as whether to offer product A or product B now becomes, how can we increase market share among millennials?

5. Clarify your objectives.

What criteria should govern this decision? This is Step #2 of SOAR™ so I'm sure you've already done this. However, whenever you are stuck in a decision, it makes sense to reexamine your objectives, priorities, and constraints. Of all the criteria, which are most important? Among those that are most important, are any of them show stoppers? Don't confuse the non-negotiable 'musts' with mere 'wants.'

6. Find more alternatives.

Another common stumbling block is inadequate alternatives. There are always more alternatives than first meet the eye. Brainstorm. Be sure to include the status quo – doing nothing. Sometimes the status quo looks pretty good compared to the alternatives under consideration, and sometimes it makes multiple alternatives look a lot better!

7. Tackle the risk and/or uncertainty.

If you are still stuck, I suspect you are mired in risk or uncertainty.

- Challenge your assumptions about what must or might happen in various scenarios.
- Don't generalize. Broad risks and worries shrink to manageable issues when you get specific.

- Figure out what you need to learn to get comfortable and go do the research. This includes learning about what could go wrong.
- Bring in an expert to help you understand the risks and best ways to mitigate or avoid those risks.

Worry paralyzes. Get to the bottom of those worries so you can make your decision and move on. If you are still stuck, delegate the decision! Obviously, you are not in a place to sort this one out.

8. The uncertain upside – escaping the black hole of indecision.

To escape the throes of indecision, you need to see your assumptions in a new light. Consider the uncertain upside. Examine worthy alternatives from the perspective of unexpected benefits. What opportunities might emerge? Suddenly, one alternative may shine. Your indecision can disappear when you discover a new dimension that wasn't captured by your list of objectives.

SOAR Through Decisions™ with a disciplined process and these pragmatic tips for greater clarity, confidence, and speed.

Where do you usually get stuck? Which tip do you think will help you the most?

Clarity Quiz – Whom Should I Invite to My Decision?

Let's flip that question around. Whom shouldn't you invite to your next decision?

1. Those with relevant knowledge and expertise.
2. Those most affected by the decision.
3. The same old team.
4. Those with the authority to decide.

Clarity of Process

If you chose #3, congratulations. Too often people make all the decisions with the same old team. This guarantees neither the quality of the decision, nor its acceptance. You need relevant knowledge and expertise to make a smart decision. You need to include representatives of those affected if you hope to have your decision accepted. Those affected are also likely to have relevant knowledge, of course. And it makes little sense to discuss a decision without the authority to decide.

In Conclusion – How Do You Make Smart Decisions Quickly?

SOAR Through Decisions™ with these four steps:

1. S – Statement of the decision you want to make. Spell it out to get everyone on the same page.
2. O – Objectives that will guide your choice of alternatives. Define these limitations, priorities, and decision criteria before debating alternatives.
3. A – Alternatives from which you will choose. There are always more alternatives than you first think.
4. R – Risks involved with the favored alternatives. Decide if you can live with them or figure out how to minimize or eliminate them.

Be disciplined and you will make better, faster decisions that create ownership, commitment, and confidence.

Clarity for Planning

"If your plans are rarely implemented,
your plans aren't the problem."
Ann Latham

Remember that the plan is not the point. The plan is just a tool to help you achieve results. Don't let the accuracy, completeness, or quality of your plan become the goal.

Top Planning Mistakes

According to Dan Gilbert in *Stumbling On Happiness*, our ability to imagine things that don't exist, envision a future, and make plans distinguishes us from other forms of life because we alone have a frontal lobe. But just because we are capable of planning, doesn't mean we couldn't do it a lot better! If your plans don't always come to fruition as desired, read on!

Planning Mistake #1: Ignoring the warning signs

Plans fail. Given the assumptions, oversights, and an unpredictable future, how can they not? So why do we so often fail to plan accordingly? Why, instead, do we 'plan harder,' trying to extract more certainty from the uncertain?

The most important and most neglected aspect of planning involves identifying potential problems so you can:

- Prevent them, and,
- Be prepared for those you fail to prevent.

So, what might go wrong to derail your current plans?

Planning Mistake #2: Planning the wrong things

Some people simply plan the wrong things. There are three main reasons for this problem. The first stems from skipping the first two steps of planning. Continue reading to learn how to *DRAW Your Plans*. The second is a result of shifting attention to the awesomeness of the plan at the expense of actual results. The third is caused by thinking you can plan unfamiliar activities the same way you plan familiar activities. Read *Why Your Planning And Tracking Are Generating Nothing More Than The Illusion Of Control* for more information on these last two.

DRAW Your Plans – How to Plan for Better Results

For the average person, the act of planning involves creating a list of action items. If you've been around the block a few times, you are wise enough to want names and dates connected to each of those action items. With a good solid list in hand, you probably feel ready to plunge ahead.

What if I told you that creating that list of action items isn't the first step of planning, but the third? If you started that way, you skipped two important steps.

And what if I told you that plunging ahead once you've completed that plan means you've skipped the fourth step as well?

Skipping three of the four steps of planning is not only super common, it is a really bad habit.

DRAW Your Plans
(The Future)

Destination
Roadmap
Action
Warnings

1. D is for Destination

What are we trying to accomplish?

When planning, don't fall prey to the tendency to begin discussing actions, or actually performing actions, before you are clear about what needs to be accomplished.

- What will success look like?
- What problem are we trying to solve?
- What will be different when we are done?

Create a clear objective, destination, outcome – whatever you want to call it – before you try to pave the shortest path to that destination.

Before you can make reservations and pack your bag for a vacation, you must choose a destination. The alternative would be a mess. You could end up at the beach with skis and boots.

Clarity of Process

The same is true if you are launching a new product. Is the goal to reach new markets, to provide a new price point for existing markets, or to augment the functionality of existing products so you can increase the revenue per existing customer? These are significantly different destinations, and your choice will affect everything from product functionality to price to marketing to how you measure success and more. Before you do any more detailed planning, determine what success would look like.

2. R is for Roadmap

Once you have a Destination, you need to scope out the various dimensions of the project. These are all the different components you need to think about. You can think of these as sub-projects or intermediate destinations. The point is to nail down the big picture Roadmap so important components aren't forgotten.

For example, when developing that new product, your Roadmap might include testing the market, developing a prototype, identifying new sales channels, recruiting celebrity champions, and increasing capacity. If you were installing a new ERP system (Enterprise Resource Planning software), you wouldn't want to omit dimensions such as writing manuals, training users, transferring legacy data, or ensuring buy-in.

I remember the first time I developed software for personal computers as opposed to mainframes. I missed a whole dimension. I thought I was done, and then my boss asked me for the installation script. An installation script is the software that runs automatically to install the application, something I didn't have to worry about in the land of mainframes. And something I had totally overlooked! The point of the Roadmap is to identify all these different dimensions or sub-projects so nothing of consequence is omitted.

While developing a good Roadmap, you will be able to work backward from the destination, review your objectives, and debate various approaches before getting bogged down in the detailed steps. This will allow you to eliminate unnecessary steps and ensure nothing significant is missed.

3. A is for Action

The third step is to identify the tasks that must be accomplished. This is the step everyone understands so I won't spend much time here. Suffice it to say, you need to know:

- What.
- Who.
- When.
- How.
- How well.

The most common mistake here is stopping with the What and Who. You can put important stakes in the ground with When, but that's not all. Use When to raise priority, resource, sequence, and dependency issues as well. Than give some attention to the How and How Well, unless you simply don't care what method is used or whether your widgets are gold-plated.

4. W is for Warning Signs

Once you've got a plan that seems ready for implementation, don't skip the final step of planning: the Warning Signs. Ask the important question: What might go wrong?

Most plans fail, and the reasons for failure are not usually all that surprising. At the very least, plans rarely turn out exactly as planned. The problem is that few people stop to ask what could go wrong. Just as a good defensive driver gives wide berth to an erratic driver, you must be wary of plans. You need to identify potential problems and then figure out how to minimize the likelihood of encountering those problems (preventive action) and prepare yourself for the eventuality should they occur despite your best efforts to avoid them (contingent action).

DRAW Your Plans with discipline from start to finish, and you are far more likely to see them succeed.

The Importance of Identifying Potential Problems

While working with a Fortune 100 company that suffered enormously costly and embarrassing delays, I rattled off a slew of reasons why their production plan had been loaded with opportunity for disaster. I told them they were the perfect example of skipping the final step of *DRAW Your Plans*. With a sly grin, the VP told me that they absolutely had identified a whole host of potential problems. Then, he added sheepishly, they just never bothered to do anything with the list!

So let's look at this step in a little more detail. The first step is to ask what might go wrong. Make a list. Draw on past experience, but also anticipate new problems. A common mistake is to concentrate only on what has gone wrong in the past. Get a little creative here and really brainstorm what might go wrong.

Focus your resources wisely

You can't prevent all problems, nor eliminate all causes. Thus, once you have a list of potential problems, rate each according to seriousness and likelihood.

- Which problems would be most serious if they did occur?
- Which problems are most likely to occur?

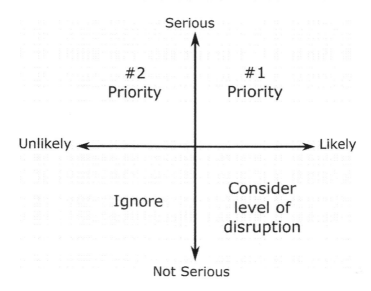

Serious and likely problems deserve the most serious consideration. These are your #1 priority.

Serious problems, even when unlikely, still deserve serious consideration. These are your #2 priority.

Ignore any potential problems that are neither likely nor serious.

The remainder, likely problems that aren't serious, might be worth ignoring. But before you do that, consider the potential level of disruption for both you and the customer should these problems actually occur.

Clarity of Process

What can you do to prevent these problems?

Here are the first set of questions to ask for each significant potential problem:

- Can we live with this risk? If we can't live with the risk, we need to prevent it or minimize its likelihood, its impact, or both
- To prevent a problem, we must eliminate its cause. What might cause the problem that concerns us?
- What preventive actions can we take to eliminate the cause of the potential problem?
- If we can't eliminate the cause, how might we reduce the likelihood of encountering this problem or the seriousness of its impact?

For example, suppose you have an important early morning appointment tomorrow. One potential problem you desperately want to avoid is being late. Being late could have myriad possible causes, so let's take them one at a time so you can choose suitable preventive actions.

- You could oversleep. To prevent oversleeping, you could go to bed early and set two alarms.
- You could also be late because you wrote down the wrong time. To be sure you have the right time, you could call to confirm the appointment the day before.
- Additional causes of lateness include wardrobe problems, traffic, parking challenges, and wrong turns. The best way to prevent all of these potential causes from making you late is to select your clothes the night before so you can get dressed while half asleep and allow yourself plenty of extra time.

And if things go wrong anyway?

Should a problem occur despite your preventive efforts, you need contingent actions:

- What might you be able to do to reduce the impact?

- How could you resolve the immediate situation?
- How would you minimize broader damage?

Consider several recent airline debacles where bad weather left people trapped on airplanes on the tarmac for hours, stranded in cramped airports, and delayed for days. Now obviously airlines can't prevent bad weather, but they can certainly have contingency plans! Leaving people trapped on the tarmac for many hours suggests zero contingency planning at the airport level.

The ripple effect, which left planes in all the wrong places and unable to get back on schedule once weather conditions improved, is indicative of terrible contingency planning at the system level. This complete lack of contingency planning resulted in miserable customers and significant damage to the airline's reputation and shareholders.

How Will You Know When Things Have Gone Wrong?

This may seem like a dumb question, but things often go wrong long before they become obvious. Once they become obvious, much of the damage is often already done. The challenge is to recognize that things are going wrong early enough to trigger your contingency plans so they can minimize the damage.

Joe, a Sales Manager for a custom manufacturing company, wanted to increase sales. He decided to institute a new sales commission structure. Being dutifully wary, he identified potential problems up front. One of those problems was that his team might start taking unprofitable business to earn bigger commissions. To prevent the problem, he reminded his team regularly to work closely with the engineers and ensure all jobs met the profitability goals. As a contingent action, he told them that if profits eroded, he would cancel the new commission plan. The problem was that he didn't monitor what was happening carefully enough. By the time he realized he needed to take contingent action and cancel the new commissions, profits were already seriously eroded.

Clarity of Process

To prevent late contingent actions, you need to create triggers by answering these questions:

- Who will be in a position to detect the problem as early as possible?
- At what point do they need to take action?

You have to know what to look for, how to monitor, and the criteria for activating any contingency plan.

For one final perfect example of skipping the big W – Warning Signs of planning, consider Wells Fargo. The company set new goals so that employees would increase sales by opening more customer accounts. Unfortunately, they pushed employees so hard that many of them created fake accounts for customers in order to make their numbers. This fraudulent behavior was:

- Not anticipated.
- Not prevented.
- Not recognized.
- Not handled honestly and openly once recognized.

I think it is safe to say that no one made an effort to identify potential problems, establish preventive or contingent actions, or set triggers so they could recognize the emerging problem promptly. Such a perfect example of failed planning!

Problems happen. Those who are on top of the game anticipate and prevent a good deal of them. Those who skip the final step are blind-sided again and again.

One Incredibly Costly Mistake You Make Over and Over Again

My clients represent for profits and nonprofits from more than 40 industries, and there is one incredibly costly mistake they all make repeatedly. I see it in organizations as they are about to embark on major change initiatives, as well as in simple decisions at weekly staff meetings. It occurs at the executive level as well as every other level in the organization. It is rampant in enormous organizations as well as small organizations. And yet, it is so simple to fix.

In a nutshell, the problem is a failure to establish a starting point. To find common ground. To establish a shared understanding of where things stand and what factors are most important in planning next steps.

Failure to establish a starting point is like asking Google Maps for directions with location services turned off. The app can't possibly help you get to your destination if it doesn't know where you are to start with. And your staff can't either.

At the beginning of any project, or even a simple decision at a staff meeting, the mistake typically manifests itself in immediately trying to head down a particular path without first agreeing on where things stand, on whether a problem or an opportunity exists, and on what success would look like.

If everyone has a different starting position – and they most certainly do – you will struggle to make progress. At best, you will have confusion, each step will be twice as hard as it needs to be, and many steps forward will be followed by two steps backward. You will go round and round on decisions. You'll argue over what is in scope and what is on or off the table. You won't be using shared criteria to guide decisions. Some people will be driven by fear. Others will unconsciously lean away or drag their feet for reasons they don't fully understand. You will struggle to keep discussions focused and productive. Energy will ebb and resentments will grow. And that's the best case.

Clarity of Process

At worst, the project proceeds for months and then implodes. Disagreements glossed over early, rear their ugly heads and, suddenly, progress is impossible. I've seen this happen with product launches, engagement programs, and major strategic initiatives. It is common, costly, and so unnecessary!

A nonprofit client of mine was heading down the road to implosion when I got involved. As I sat in on a board meeting, someone identified an important decision he thought would need to be made. Objections erupted. "We made that decision following considerable research two years ago!" I don't care what happened two years ago. If half the board believes the issue is open and in scope, it does no good to try to slam the door on it by turning to the past. This is a perfect example of disagreement about the starting point! Had we ignored this gap and favored either side, it could have sunk the whole project.

The same problem can affect even small decisions at a weekly staff meeting. In the best case scenario, diving in without the right starting point just wastes time. You go round and round, confusing risks with objectives and resistance with alternatives. In the worst case, you erode trust and confidence as people struggle to be heard.

By clarifying your starting point and the decision at hand, you save tremendous time and prevent a host of extraneous explanations and unnecessary confusion.

I've worked on many complex and sensitive decisions involving disjointed groups with little in common. I've taken them from distrust, misunderstanding, and wholesale animosity to unanimous conclusions, despite requiring significant change and compromise from all parties. In every case, I can say that a good part of my success stemmed from finding the right starting point before diving in. If you want a group to embrace a shared outcome, you will get there faster and more reliably if you start in the right place and find common ground. Some good questions to ask include:

- What are we trying to accomplish?
- Why do we want to change?

- What decision are we trying to make?
- What decisions have been made already?
- What factors should govern our decisions?
- What's negotiable and what isn't?
- What scares us and what gives us hope?
- What would success look like?

Finding that shared starting point is absolutely critical if you want a smooth process that garners commitment and drives real results.

Why SMART Goals Aren't So Smart

SMART goals – Specific, Measurable, Attainable, Relevant, and Timely – are all the rage, but are they smart?

A smart goal is one that will be achieved. And if you want your goals to be achieved, these five SMART factors have several fatal flaws.

First, the SMART factors don't do much to ensure goals are important to the organization. 'Relevant' is a weak statement of importance. Any goal worth defining and tracking should make a significant impact on the success of the organization.

Second, the SMART factors say nothing about the individual who needs to achieve the goal. You can't tell me a particular goal is equally smart for any number of different individuals. People are not interchangeable and therefore the goals assigned to them can't be either.

Third, the SMART factors ignore characteristics that increase the odds that a goal will be achieved. They help managers put good, strong stakes in the ground, but they don't do much for those who must execute.

Fourth, the SMART factors do little to gain the commitment of those who must act or change their behavior, another critical component for success.

Clarity of Process

Thus, it is time to take a new approach. It is time to bring SANITY to goal setting. Success is far more likely if you create important goals that will be achieved. Let SANITY be your new guide to setting goals.

SANITY Goal Setting

1. S is for Supported

If you don't support people by providing adequate resources, time, authority, guidance, feedback, and follow-up, they are not likely to achieve their goals. Many a SMART goal has withered on the vine, fed only with wishful thinking and no real support.

2. A is for Appropriate

Creating goals that are appropriate for a particular individual's skill, knowledge, talents, and workload is a significant factor needed for success. Nothing increases productivity and quality more than matching the task to someone with the right capabilities and inclination.

3. N is for Negotiable

Success requires commitment and you won't get commitment if you make demands and leave people feeling they are being set up for failure. This is especially true for stretch goals and situations outside the employee's full control. However, if you involve the employee in goal setting, make it clear that the point is to excel, both individually and collectively (not to punish or pit one against another), and acknowledge that adjustments may be necessary to reflect new information, shifting priorities, and other crystal ball inadequacies, employees are much more likely to step up to the challenge and make that critical commitment.

4. I is for Important

Don't establish any goals that aren't important. Every goal should have a significant positive impact on the organization.

5. T is for Tangible

If the employee can visualize nothing but a giant, amorphous mountain of complexity and barriers, success is unlikely. But if the employee can see at least a vague path to the desired destination and a clear, concrete first step, the odds of success increase dramatically. If the first and subsequent steps reveal additional tangible, concrete steps, the goal is practically in the bag.

6. Y is for Yes

No matter how important you may think a goal is, progress will be minimal unless the implementer believes the goal is valuable. If the individual can honestly say, "Yes, I understand and I agree that this is very important to me and the company," you are much more likely to get the commitment and energy that is needed for success.

Well-defined goals are important, which is the intention of SMART. But bring a little SANITY to the process if you want to achieve and exceed more goals and set the right *destination* for your planning process.

The Second Most Important Question to Ask Daily

"How will we know when we are done?"

When I meet with prospective clients, I ask them first about their objectives. My second question is, "How will we know when we are done?" I need to be certain we are in complete agreement as to what we would see if we were making progress and how we would know if we were finished. Since I don't simply deliver prepackaged content and since I am totally outcome focused, I can't operate any other way.

What I don't understand is why anyone would want to operate any other way.

73

Clarity of Process

When you launch a big employee engagement program, how will you know when you are done? And don't tell me you will survey all employees, scrutinize the results, and identify needed changes. Those are tasks and inputs, not outcomes. Will attrition decrease? Will employees volunteer for greater responsibility or encourage their friends to join the company? Will you be called into fewer low level decisions? What would constitute real evidence that you have engaged your employees?

When you send employees to training, how will you know it was effective? What will you expect to see as evidence of success? Where will you expect to see your employees demonstrating their new skills?

When you hold a meeting, how will you know when you are finished? Do you know what must be different when it ends or do you rely on the clock to tell you it is over?

When you work alone at your desk on anything, how will you know when you are finished? What will success look like in one hour?

My clients don't pay me to wander and the company isn't paying you to wander either. Whether you are looking out an hour, a day, a week, a month or a year, you have to know what success looks like if you hope to achieve it effectively and efficiently.

Increase your clarity with this question, the second most important question to ask regularly:

- **How will we know when we are done?**

What is the most important question?

- **What are we trying to accomplish?**

Two critical questions. Fourteen words. Memorize them. Use them frequently!

Clear Distinctions: Starting vs. Wandering In

I do it myself when I'm not careful. 'Wandering in' is a wasteful habit that takes three forms:

1. You start a task without a clear destination, a clear sense of what will be different when you are done.
2. You start a task without a clear route, a clear sense of specific steps that will get you to your destination.
3. You don't really start the task. You check your email, look up something on the Internet, finish reading an article, make some notes about something else, schedule an appointment, answer the telephone, get a cup of coffee, etc.

In the first two cases, you get lost in the task. In the third, you get lost in between tasks. Whether you succumb to one, two, or all three forms of wandering in, you will lose significant time. Next thing you know, half an hour or more has passed and you are still wandering around in or between tasks.

Starting, on the other hand, involves an intentional decision to launch yourself down a clear path to a specific finish line. You glance at the clock, set an end time in your mind, push everything else aside, and then sprint toward that destination.

The difference is enormous. Starting is tremendously effective. Wandering in is not.

Starting requires discipline and the habit of being intentional and specific about your goal, next step, and expected completion time. If you save the wandering for your leisure hours, you will be amazed by how many more leisure hours you will have!

Why Your Planning And Tracking Are Generating Nothing More Than The Illusion Of Control

During my early days in the corporate world, one of my jobs included developing the software that synchronized and backed up all the data needed to control the generation and transmission of power for Great Britain. The project manager made the rounds every Friday to update his Gantt chart. He stepped through each activity and asked me for an updated percent complete. I struggled with this exercise and finally, when my tasks hit 67%, I refused to play. Despite my long list of open tasks marked two-thirds complete, I promised him we'd be finished on time.

This tracking ritual continued weekly, and every Friday he could hardly contain his anger with me. He told me my group was going to ruin the whole project. I told him not to worry. My promises did nothing to relieve his anxiety.

Meanwhile, all the other leads were marching steadily toward the finish line and keeping him happy. 70%. 75%. 78%. 80%. 82%. To increase the pressure on laggards like me, the charts were posted on the wall. Practically everyone was in the 90s and my group still showed 67%.

The day before our deadline, my group finished. All our software components worked with each other and passed the system tests with flying colors. Just as I promised. It was time to mark the boxes complete and I did.

The project manager was still unhappy. Why? Because we were the only group that finished on time. The others were trying to squeeze new integers between 98 and 99%.

Why Did I Refuse To Update The Numbers?

I wouldn't play because it was a meaningless game. We were doing things we had never done before. When you conclude that you are 90% complete, you are assuming that you understand everything left to be done and that all will go exactly as expected. All it takes is one false assumption to throw a wrench in the works, and some of those wrenches can be enormous. It doesn't matter how many hours you've put in. It doesn't matter how many lines of code you've written. What matters is whether all the pieces work together correctly in the end. This is why the first 90% of coding usually takes 90% of the time and the remaining 10% takes the other 90% of the time (Tom Cargill, Bell Labs).

How Did I Know We Would Finish On Time?

My group finished on time because instead of focusing on:

- Checking things off a list,
- Mistaking the plan for the goal, and
- Trying to look good.

We focused on:

- Our software,
- The deadline, and
- The things that stood between us and our deadline.

To understand the difference better, consider the following chart. The left-hand side represents tasks that are familiar to you. These are things you've done before, at least mostly. The right-hand side represents tasks that are unfamiliar. They may be completely new to you or even completely new period. The top half represents simple tasks and the bottom is for complex tasks.

The trouble with plans

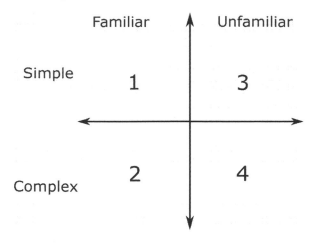

Quadrant 1 covers the simple and familiar parts of the plan. You might be able to do some of these in your sleep. Quadrant 2 planning makes you work and think harder, but they aren't mysteries. These tasks might require a lot of care and/or coordination with others, but they don't require a rocket scientist. Quadrant 3 tasks are pretty simple, but since they are unfamiliar to you, you don't know what you don't know. Quadrant 4 tasks are where calling in the rocket scientists might be a good idea. You've got both complexity and unknowns. These tasks will require some serious learning, heavy-duty experimentation, and significant coordination, as well as some luck.

Why Traditional Planning And Tracking Fails

Think about traditional planning and tracking practices relative to these four quadrants.

- Which quadrants are most easily planned? 1 is obviously the easiest. Next comes 2. Then 3. Last, 4.
- Which are most accurately planned? 1, 2, 3 and 4. In that order.
- If you want an accurate schedule, where will you spend the most time? Ah, here is a slight change! 2, 1, 3 and then 4 is the order. Accuracy is possible with quadrant 2 tasks, but it takes work and time.
- If you want to show quick progress, either to get off to a good start or to make up for lost time, where would you focus your attention? 1, 2, and then 3 and 4.

It's only natural. Traditional planning and tracking practices draw attention to 1, 2, 3, and then 4. In that order. But the consequences are horrible!

- Which quadrant is most likely to blow the schedule out of the water? 4, 3, 2, and then 1. In that order!
- Which quadrant is most likely to blow the budget sky high? 4, 3, 2, and then 1.
- Which quadrant is most likely to be responsible for creating unhappy customers? 4, 3, 2, and then 1.

Most plans simply create the illusion of control and distract from the true priorities.

1. Don't Let The Plan Become The Objective

Plans are just tools. They are not the goal. Checked off boxes are not results. Don't let the plan become more important than real progress.

Clarity of Process

2. Avoid The Questions That Make People Tell You What You Want To Hear But Not What You Need To Hear

Most project managers think they can get results by holding people accountable with questions such as:

- Are you on schedule?
- Are you on budget?
- Are you going to meet the performance requirements?

How do you think most people answer these questions? They say yes, scramble off, and hope they will never have to reverse their position. The illusion of control is sustained!

3. Make The Unfamiliar Familiar

The familiar tasks are so easy to plan you barely need a plan. If you want to control the schedule, budget, and quality, concentrate on learning so the unfamiliar becomes familiar. Once the unfamiliar is familiar, planning is easy! To speed this transition, adopt a 'defensive driving' mindset:

- What have we learned?
- What do we still need to learn?
- What are we taking for granted?
- How do you know you will finish on time?
- How do we know we can meet the customer requirements?

These questions take the focus off the plan and put the attention on the only things that matter: the goal, the deadline, and the obstacles that stand between you and your deadline.

Don't support the Illusion of Control with traditional planning and tracking. Devote your attention instead to the unfamiliar tasks and the learning needed to make them familiar.

Abolish Priorities!

Did you know that almost no one made the word 'priority' plural before the 1950s? Having multiple priorities probably made about as much sense as describing something as 'very unique.' Something is either unique or it isn't. And something is either the priority or it isn't. Makes sense to me!

Once you have two priorities, what is the priority? And once you have two, why can't you have three? How about four? Where is the line?

We all know that if you have too many priorities, you have no priorities.

Franklin-Covey teaches that if you have 2-3 priorities, you will complete 2-3 tasks. If you have 4-10 priorities, you will complete 1-2 tasks. And if you have more than 10, you will complete none.

I'd take that a step further. At any given moment, you have to have only one priority. If you have two, you will not be able to focus and your productivity will suffer.

Try eliminating 'priorities' from your vocabulary. If you speak only of your one priority, you will:

- Be clear about what is most important right now, later today, tomorrow, as well as this month. "My priority right now is to finish this newsletter. My priority after that is to return phone calls. My priority for this quarter is to write a book." Pretty clear, eh?
- Avoid the cop-out involved with maintaining multiple 'most important' tasks.
- Improve your ability to make tough decisions.
- Make more realistic plans.
- Set a good example for others who morph priority into a plural noun that has nothing to do with priority.
- Be more productive.

Now go out into the world where 'priorities' rule, and do your best to maintain that singular focus!

Clarity Quiz – Objectives vs. Goals

I'm frequently asked about the difference between objectives and goals. My response: Who cares! This is not a distinction worthy of discussion. Let me demonstrate why this is true.

1. Do you know what you are trying to accomplish?
2. Is your definition of success sufficiently clear and specific so it will be obvious when you have achieved it? You can envision what *done* looks like?
3. Do you have a reasonable deadline from which to work backward in scheduling your work and maintaining an appropriate sense of urgency?
4. Are you committed to success? This includes knowing what is of lesser importance and when you will have to say no to ensure success.

If you can answer yes to all four, you are in good shape whether you think you have goals, objectives, both, or neither!

If you can't answer yes to all four, you are probably in trouble regardless of whether you think you have goals, objectives, both, or neither!

Debating the difference between goals and objectives is as useless as most goals and objectives because most goals and objectives don't meet these four criteria.

In Conclusion – DRAW Your Plans

DRAW Your Plans with these four steps:

1. D – Start by clarifying your Destination.
2. R – Scope out your general Roadmap so you don't neglect important components while lost in the details.
3. A – Identify the Actions needed to reach your destination.
4. W – Make a list of Warnings, everything that could go wrong so you can develop preventive and contingent action plans to reduce the risk.

And, remember, the plan is not your goal! It is merely a tool to help you succeed. Keep your eye on the real goal and concentrate on eliminating the obstacles between you and success.

Clarity for Problem Solving

"You can't solve a problem without eliminating its cause."
Ann Latham

Find the cause of the problem. You can't solve a problem without eliminating its cause! Don't throw fancy and exciting solutions like darts at a target, 99.9% of which miss the bullseye and pin money, resources, time, and energy to the wrong initiatives.

The Three Problem Solving Mistakes

Leaping to solutions is undoubtedly a familiar concept to you. I remember hearing it in my earliest working days. Despite ubiquitous admonitions to avoid leaping to solutions, it remains a huge problem. Furthermore, leaping to solutions isn't the only common mistake. Read on to learn of two others. More importantly, read on to discover a logical process for solving problems that will not only help you solve problems once and for all, but will also help you do so in synch with the brainpower of other people.

Problem Solving Mistake #1: Leaping to solutions

When something isn't working as expected, people have a tendency to start trying a variety of 'fixes.' Some 'fixes' are so exciting they eclipse all others and a new project is underway before you know it. The temptation is huge. But the likelihood of success is nearly zero. That's because you can't solve a problem without eliminating its cause.

Problem Solving Mistake #2: Confusing problems with wishes

A problem is a situation where something is not behaving the way it should. Generally speaking, there are three types of problems:

- Something has stopped working as expected. All was fine and now it isn't.
- Similar situations are not producing similar results. Some results are adequate and some aren't.
- Performance is irregular. Decent results are achieved only part of the time.

These are problems, and you deal with them by figuring out what has changed or what is different about the circumstances that produce inadequate results.

However, don't call it a problem when something doesn't measure up to your expectations and never has! That is called wishful thinking.

Problem Solving Mistake #3: Solving unimportant problems

Not all problems are worth solving. Some things quit working or never achieve reliability. Some behaviors don't change as hoped and some projects are never completely implemented. And sometimes it doesn't matter! Don't let curiosity or compulsiveness drive you to solve a problem that is of little consequence in the grand scheme of things!

SPOT Remover For Problems – How To Solve Problems Better and Faster

I am one of those people who can't go to sleep at night until a problem is solved. I discovered this in math classes long before majoring in the subject in college. Heck, I discovered this as a small child every time I got my hands on one of those tangles of metal that can be separated into two parts only with the right twists and turns. As a software engineer, I continued to solve problems. All night long, if necessary. As a consultant, I am still solving problems, though now those problems involve business challenges, often quite twisted and tangled! And I've got to tell you, no matter how good I've gotten to be at solving problems, I still pay attention to process. Actually, let me flip that around. My success at solving problems is undoubtedly a result of disciplined process.

If you want to solve problems effectively, especially when working with other people, a disciplined process[2] is invaluable. My *SPOT Remover for Problems* will save you time and help you avoid 'solutions' that aren't really solutions because they don't work.

1. S is for Specifics

Specifics come first. You can't solve a problem if you aren't clear about what exactly the problem is.

A problem is a situation where something is not behaving the way it should. As mentioned above, there are three types of problems. Let's look at each in more detail:

---

[2] Kepner-Tregoe in the New Rational Manager introduce an excellent process for problem solving. My work is influenced by their clear thinking.

1. **Something has stopped working as expected.** All was fine and now it isn't. The trick to solving these problems is to determine what has changed causing the change in performance. Something has to have changed. What is different now compared to when results were consistently good enough?

2. **Seemingly identical situations are producing different results** and some of those results just aren't good enough. The trick, in this case, is to determine in what way these situations aren't identical. You may think the machines, processes, skills, environments, etc., are all identical, but if you are getting different results, something is different about the circumstances. If you find those differences, you can eliminate them.

3. **Performance is irregular.** Good results are achieved part of the time but inadequate results occur at other times. The trick is to distinguish the circumstances that produce good results from those that don't so you can replicate those that do and eliminate those that don't.

The two most powerful problem solving questions are:

1. What has changed?
2. What are the differences between the circumstances producing good results and those producing inadequate results?

Be specific. To avoid general 'fixes' that miss the mark, you have to know exactly what has stopped working or what is different about the circumstances when things work well and when they don't. Think in terms of changes and distinctions.

2. P is for Possible Causes

You can't solve a problem without eliminating its cause. If you haven't short-changed Step #1, you now know the specifics that define your problem and are ready to identify possible causes. Be open-minded. Look carefully at the evidence you've compiled.

Clarity of Process

- What is causing your problem?
- What kinds of causes have you encountered in the past?
- What might have caused the changes you discovered?
- What is behind the distinctions you discovered?

Be sure you find the real cause or your 'solutions' will miss the mark.

3. O is for Options

The third step of problem solving is to identify possible options for eliminating the cause of the problem. Some people call these possible solutions, but most aren't solutions so let's not call them that. They are simply possibilities. Options to consider.

After you generate ideas for eliminating the cause of the problem, you must pick the option you think most likely to succeed. Only once you show success can you be sure you have a solution!

Thus, generate good options for eliminating the cause and pick the one you think is most likely to work.

4. T is for Test

Once you are pretty sure you've identified the cause of the problem and a good method for eliminating that cause, it is time to test your hypothesis. How can you prove that you've identified the real cause and chosen an option that will actually eliminate that cause? Make your test as narrow as possible before you apply a potential solution to a situation that affects many people, processes, and locations.

If the problem recurs with your 'fix' in place, you either:

- Did not identify the cause.
- Did not eliminate the cause.

Time to go back to the drawing board! You can't solve a problem without eliminating the cause. Use *SPOT* to bring clarity and discipline to your problem solving. You will save time, solve problems once and for all, and avoid expensive roll-outs of ineffective 'solutions.'

Killing a Killer-Bad Habit

At the beginning of a recent strategic planning project, I used a survey to get the lay of the land, generate ideas, and stimulate the thinking of those who would be involved in the process. I asked several questions about cause and needs, for example: What are the barriers to customer success? What customer need is no one meeting?

Many of the respondents leaped over cause and need, and went straight to 'solutions.' For example:

What are the barriers to customer success?
"We need to provide a more complete set of offerings such as ..."

What customer need goes unserved?
"We should modify our products to ..."

I am certain that these respondents have no idea that they did not answer my questions. This leaping to solutions is not at all uncommon. Actually, it is ridiculously common and is the number one problem-solving mistake that people make.

But this is a bad habit because you can't satisfy your customers if you don't take the time to understand their needs. If your first reaction involves your organization's capabilities or desired capabilities, you will miss the mark every time.

Furthermore, you can't solve a problem if you don't remove the underlying cause. What is preventing your customers from achieving greater success? What is preventing your customers from embracing your products? What do your customers need that no one else is providing? The cause of their problems may be your path to opportunity. (See *10 Ways To Stand Out From The Crowd And Win In The Game Of Business.*)

Organizations waste ridiculous quantities of money and time developing products and systems that miss the mark because they skip over cause and need and jump right to solutions.

10 Reasons Leaders Get Dragged Into Problems Unnecessarily And What To Do About It

My clients, readers, and audiences complain frequently about getting dragged into issues that ought to be resolved without their help. Every time an issue is escalated one, two, three, even more levels, the cost is significant. "Why can't people just solve these problems themselves?" they ask.

Well, you can't eliminate a problem without eliminating its cause so here are the 10 most frequent causes of unnecessary escalation.

1. Unclear Priorities

Employees can't make decisions without understanding the criteria that should govern those decisions. Sometimes those criteria are project specific (e.g., requirements, customer expectations, cost/schedule trade-offs) and sometimes they are company wide and involve strategic priorities (priority accounts, product life-cycle plans, customer service expectations, quality/schedule trade-offs, etc.) Without clarity, employees often need to escalate what could be simple decisions.

2. Unclear Options

Every decision involves choosing among options. Employees often hit roadblocks because they don't know what options they have. Sometimes it's a matter of policy – "Can I issue a discount or rebate to a customer?" Or it could be insufficient information about technology or downstream processes – "Will I hose up the system if they enter data a day late?" And sometimes the issue involves subject matter expertise – "Is this hole going to be too big now? Can we get the accuracy needed if we make this substitution?" Depending on the situation, ensuring clarity of options may require training on company policy, technical training, better customer requirements, process training, and quick access to experts and reference resources.

3. Unclear Responsibilities

Sometimes employees know exactly how to handle a situation, but they don't dare. Why? Because they are afraid they will step on someone's toes or ruffle someone's feathers. Clear responsibilities solve this problem.

4. Mixed Signals

Too often, a company says one thing and does another. The most common example is when employees are told that quality trumps cost and schedule, but then when they hold up a shipment due to concerns about quality, they suffer everything from dagger eyes to official demerits on their next performance review. You can't expect employees to make decisions when they can feel the wind coming at them from all directions.

5. Controversial Priorities Or Policies

Most employees will refuse to take responsibility for a decision based on priorities or policies they find disagreeable. "You want to fire him for such a trivial reason, than you go ahead and do it. I'm not." "You want to ship that motorcycle without wheels, go right ahead. I won't." "You can tell him he needs to work all weekend because you screwed up. I'm not doing it."

Clarity of Process

6. Fear

Fear paralyzes. Fearful employees would much rather others made decisions, especially tough decisions. Have you made them fearful? Do you shoot the messenger? Do you broadcast mixed signals? Do you seek blame instead of lessons and changes that will prevent a recurrence?

7. Lack Of Confidence

Employees may be fully aware of priorities, options, and responsibilities, but still doubt they know enough. A lack of confidence leaves qualified employees searching for confirmation when they could be taking action. Build their confidence by confirming their knowledge and making it clear they are as ready to make decisions as the people they typically turn to.

8. Inadequate Understanding Of Risks

"But what could go wrong?" Some people neglect to ask this question. You should applaud the ones that do, because good, confident decisions require an understanding of the potential impact of those decisions. Too often, leaders tell employees what to do, but not why. Always explain why so that you build the awareness, knowledge, and confidence to make decisions without unnecessary escalation.

9. No Authority

Nothing wastes time and degrades employees like a senseless search for a signature or nod. Once employees understand priorities, options, and risks, let them make the decision!

10. "Above My Pay Grade"

Big, risky decisions, especially if compounded by any of the other factors, may simply wind up above the pay grade of the employees on the spot. They don't want that kind of responsibility and they aren't paid to take that kind of responsibility. These aren't the people who will brighten up and thank you if you suggest they step up to the plate. Pay attention. Find someone who feels up to the task and make those responsibilities clear.

If you've been paying attention, you will have noticed that the source of unnecessary escalation is always connected to decisions. That's because it's the decisions that slow us down and give us opportunities to take the wrong fork. To avoid unnecessary escalation, you need to focus on the decisions. Where are they? Whose are they? What do those decision makers need to keep things moving quickly and effectively? Support necessary decisions at the source to reduce unnecessary escalation. If necessary go back and look at how to *SOAR Through Decisions*™ to get clarity.

So Much To Do, So Little Time!

Time management is a perpetual rage. It conjures up images of calendars, personal planners, and smart phones. When we have too much to do and too little time, we flail about for a new system that will suddenly lasso the hands of the clock and give us control.

But time cannot be managed. It is ourselves that we must manage. Tools like calendars and planners are helpful, but for the best results, we must consider a variety of obstacles that prevent us from focusing on and completing the important tasks while dismissing everything else. And, as always, to solve any problem, you have to eliminate its cause. What's preventing you from feeling productive and successful?

Clarity of Process

1. **Are you clear about your top priorities?**
   It is better to move a few things forward a mile than to nudge the multitude forward an inch, or worse, shuffle them side to side without any measurable progress? Decide what most needs doing. If there are too many priorities, nothing is a priority.

2. **Are you so overwhelmed that you don't know where to start?**
   Or is the fear that something is about to drop through the cracks leaving you too stressed to focus? A good place to start is to make a list of all the things you must do. Once everything is on paper, your mind will be less cluttered and more able to take stock. You can then identify priorities and deadlines.

3. **Are you distracted constantly by piles of projects and random reminders of things requiring attention?**
   If so, you either need to clean up the mess or move to a clean office. Projects belong in folders in file cabinets or in notebooks on the shelf. Reminders belong on calendars or lists. If you get things out of your mind by recording them in a good system consisting of a calendar, lists, and folders, you can add new thoughts quickly and focus on tasks with the comfort of knowing that everything is under control. If things aren't under control, your productivity will suffer dreadfully.

4. **Do you allow yourself to be distracted unnecessarily?**
   Most interruptions can be blocked by turning off the email notifier, silencing the ringer on your phone, and closing your door. While some interruptions are unavoidable, most are too readily welcomed. Whether seeking an excuse for a break or confirmation of our importance to others, we are often unwilling to shut out the distractions for any length of time.

5. **Do you distract yourself constantly just because you are so used to being wired and distracted?**
   Don't laugh. When you operate in a state of constant interruption, you begin to interrupt yourself. It may be time for you to replace the distraction habit with purposeful self-discipline. Before you start the next task on your list, state the outcome and allotted time aloud. Then do nothing else until you are finished. Set a timer if you must and don't get out of your chair or turn to another task until you finish or the alarm sounds.

6. **Do you believe in the importance of the task?**
   If you can't understand why a task is important, you won't be motivated to complete it. Revisit the rationale. Maybe it isn't important. Maybe this is one task you can eliminate. On the other hand, a new-found sense of the importance may be just what you need to pull the trigger.

7. **Do you find yourself procrastinating despite believing in the importance of the task?**
   If so, your quandary may be in the means, not the end. Either you don't believe the route leads to your destination or you don't even have a route in mind. To make progress, you need to have both a general, believable approach as well as a specific, reasonable next step. It is hard to make progress if all you see is a mountain; it is easy to make progress if you see the first step of a stairway to a valuable destination. Replace nebulous To-Do list tasks with specific, concrete next steps.

8. **Do you have the knowledge, skill, and confidence needed to complete the task?**
   You may legitimately need help or you may be agonizing over nothing. What is your concern? What specifically do you need to know to move forward? What is really at stake if you make a mistake? If you get specific about what you need in order to proceed, it will be easier to find the appropriate answers and support. If you get specific about the risk you face, it will be easier to reduce or live with that risk.

9. **Do you dwell in the land of diminishing returns?**
   If you have a tendency toward perfectionism, consciously target an appropriate level of quality. Thirty percent or sixty percent may be sufficient. The last twenty percent is almost always worth less than the effort required to achieve it. As a matter of fact, the difference between a product that is eighty percent ready and one that is 'perfect' is often detectable only by the creator.

10. **Do you always add and never subtract?**
    It is harder to decide what not to do than to simply add to the list. But if you keep adding, something has to give. Would you rather make a conscious decision by taking something off the list or let the squeezing and chopping just happen?

11. **Do you allow others to suck up your time or expand your list?**
    Some people are wizards at handing off tasks to the unsuspecting or unassertive. Be alert and willing to say no. Others are famous for seeking support, asking questions, or just chatting. Sharpen your critical thinking by helping them get to the point quickly.

12. **Are you the right person for the task?**
    When your talent and personality, not to mention priorities, are not matched to the task, your productivity and energy will both run low. Unless you have a particular need to develop the required skill or knowledge, delegate or outsource for the best results and the best use of your time.

13. **Or perhaps, you would simply rather do something else and not the top priority with its obvious value and that you could easily do if you had the self-discipline.**
    Get it off your plate along with the negative feelings you derive from this situation. Decide how long the task should take. Put it on the calendar, preferably for first thing some morning. Set the timer when that time comes. Block out all distractions and focus until you finish. Then reward yourself before moving on to the next project.

Without looking at the specific obstacles to your own productivity, your efforts to improve are likely to be misguided. What is preventing you from focusing on and completing the important tasks right now?

If It's Stupid, Stop Doing It!

Within one two-day period, I encountered four examples of clients jumping through hoops to manage dysfunctional situations rather than fixing the situations.

- Changing time sheets to accurately reflect vacation and sick time in a system that requires employees to record their work hours before the week even begins.
- Struggling to make an unnecessary standing meeting appear effective rather than canceling the meeting.
- Plotting to involve someone, somehow just to avoid perennial conflict.
- Creating yet another beautiful plan when the track record is paved with dusty plans and no execution.

Dissimilar as these are, they are all examples of wasting time and money unnecessarily and repeatedly by not addressing the underlying problem.

If your plans are rarely implemented, the plan isn't the problem. If obsolete responsibility assignments make you tiptoe around an individual, the responsibilities need to be clarified or changed. If you've got a meeting in search of a purpose, cancel it. If your systems are cumbersome and causing rework, change the systems. Bite the bullet and fix the underlying problem. It may take a little time and courage, but it makes no sense to suffer repeatedly at the hand of a dysfunctional situation.

Clarity of Process

Not sure what those situations are or how to fix them? The first clues are frustration and fog. The next time a situation is annoying, painful, or clearly unsatisfactory, no matter how many times you've plowed through it before, ask why. Why are we doing this? Why are we in this situation? Why aren't we succeeding? Why is this so hard? Ask "Why?" until you gain clarity.

Clarity makes problems evident, solutions specific, and systems simpler. If it hurts, stop doing it!

How Can I Think More Quickly On My Feet?

"Dear Ann, I loved your webinar on meetings, your newsletters are so informative, and I have a couple of your books too! What I could really use is some advice on thinking quickly on my feet, especially when answering to a VP or Director."

Great question! Since I couldn't recall answering this question before, I was intrigued. My reader and I exchanged a few emails so I could clarify the situation and ensure my answer was on target.

My reader works in healthcare. Since accurate communication is so important to patient care, they use a proven technique called SBAR, which stands for Situation, Background, Assessment, and Recommendation. This framework creates a structured and standardized format so that health care workers can exchange important information quickly and effectively. It creates shared clarity!

I asked my reader if she has trouble thinking quickly on her feet when responding to questions within the context of SBAR.

"No," she replied. "It is only when senior people show up and ask me questions that catch me by surprise."

By probing further, I discovered that the questions that leave her struggling are all incredibly vague. They are the equivalent of asking me what I do. Let's see, how many ways might I answer that question? I create clarity. I help my clients get better results faster. I consult, coach, and speak, I travel and read as much as I can, ... I could go on!

Consider my reader's plight:

- She is eager to be concise and helpful and waste no one's time.
- She is faced with a totally unclear question that could be answered in many ways.
- She blames herself.

What should she do?

First and foremost, she should not feel inadequate in the face of others who are unclear! That in itself will improve her ability to think more clearly!

Second, she has two choices:

1. Guess, or,
2. Ask clarifying questions.

I recommend the latter. It is much more effective than guessing someone's intent and then blathering on in the hopes of meeting particular needs.

If she were the boss and not the victim, I would add one more option to that list: learn how to create more shared clarity across the organization.

Clarity of Process

As I mentioned, SBAR creates clarity by providing a framework for communication. But it does more than improve communication. It also provides a framework for thinking. By stepping through the four step process, people can be much more thorough and intentional. "Have I covered the current situation adequately? What background information might we be missing given our most recent findings?" On top of that, the SBAR framework improves the ability of others to supplement or question opinions and facts at each step. The result is safer, better, and faster health care decisions.

While SBAR is a very specific tool for a very specific industry, tools like this don't have to be so narrowly focused. I teach my clients to *SOAR Through Decisions*™. SOAR™ works with any decision and, like SBAR, it improves communication, thinking, and the ability to interact effectively with others. The result is better, faster decisions. You can read more about the *SOAR Through Decisions*™ process in the section on Decisions.

You can also take advantage of the *SPOT Remover for Problems*, my framework for removing problems – once and for all. Like SBAR and SOAR™, it creates shared clarity by getting everyone on the same page, establishing a shared language, and providing a logical process to better solutions.

Tools like SOAR™ and SPOT help my clients save significant time while also improving results. They are great examples of the power of shared clarity.

Want to help everyone think more quickly on their feet and create clarity in the moment? Focus on creating shared clarity! The benefits are better results faster with far greater confidence and commitment!

Clarity Quiz – Which Problem Solving Step Do People Most Frequently Miss?

Which step of the problem solving process do people most often short-change?

1. Specifics – They don't take enough time to understand the specific conditions under which the problem does and doesn't occur.
2. Potential Causes – They don't really consider potential causes because they come into the problem with preconceived notions about the cause or they are already thinking about their preferred 'solution.'
3. Options – Potential solutions are options. Too often people glom onto a preferred 'solution' and never really consider other options.
4. Test – Preferred 'solutions' generate so much enthusiasm that few people stop to test.
5. All of the above.

I wish I could say that one step is generally executed well. Unfortunately, I can't. The answer is definitely #5.

The most common approach to problem solving is a disorganized meeting that involves a cursory look at the situation followed by vociferous support for pet solutions. The 'systems' people advocate for a new checklist. The HR people want to develop more training. The analytical people favor additional data collection and are subsequently ignored thanks to everyone else's impatience or fear of analysis paralysis. The skeptics scorn all ideas. And the eternal optimists are ready to lead any charge. As a result, most 'solutions' miss the mark.

In Conclusion – How Do You Solve A Problem Once and For All?

If you want to solve a problem once and for all, you must eliminate the cause. Everything else is wasted time and energy. Find the cause.

Clarity for Time Management

"You can't manage time; you can only manage yourself."
Ann Latham

Abolish the phrases:
"There is too much to do."
"There is not enough time."

Of course there is too much to do! And there will never be enough time! These are victim words that make you helpless to choose and act effectively. Abolish them today!

15 Time-Wasting Activities Corporations Encourage Daily

Success and profits come from devoting resources to activities that create value for which customers are willing to pay and minimizing resources devoted to everything else. If you are serious about improving results, you need to take a good hard look at the time you and your employees spend on the following activities:

1. **Planning** – especially the portions so familiar they barely need planning and those so unfamiliar that traditional detailed planning can only create fiction and the illusion of control. Planning is important, but plans are not a business outcome. Stop worshipping your plans and measuring success with checked-off tasks. Instead, start asking employees how they know they will finish on time.

2. **Wandering** – operating without a clear process. If you don't have a clear method, you won't take the shortest path. Pick the best path before you enter the woods! This applies to large tasks as well as the next half hour spent alone at your desk.

3. **Generalizing** – building enterprise-wide solutions to address one mistake or under-performing employee. It is so much easier to just train everyone than to figure out why things aren't working as desired! But you've got to stop doing it! You can't solve a problem without eliminating its cause.

4. **Controlling** – establishing rules, forms, formats, procedures, and other controlling structures in an effort to improve performance. That will only work if a lack of controls and structures is the root cause of disappointing performance.

5. **Reporting** – justifying time and money expended, even though it creates zero value and prevents next to zero problems. Reporting is traditional, hard to avoid, and the most insidious of all *Treadmill Verbs*™! You can report forever. There is no way to know when you are done!

6. **Reviewing** – looking something over without any idea whether the goal is to ensure strategic value, comprehensibility, completeness, accuracy, or the absence of typos and grammatical mistakes.

7. **Documenting** – because if we write it all down, everyone will finally get it and there will be no excuse for not doing it! Sure. I used to believe that. It doesn't work.

8. **Discussing** – so everyone feels heard. And not manipulated? A fair, transparent decision-making process is a far better choice.

9. **Guessing** – responding to vague requests and writing email messages without a clear understanding of your audience. Everyone must learn to stop and create clarity in the moment! Ask clarifying questions!

10. **Waiting** – especially for busy people who aren't getting back to you – and never will because it isn't a lack of time keeping them from getting back to you! More likely, it's a lack of clarity about what you need and/or what you requested.

11. **Shuffling** – paper, priorities, To-Do lists, and plans instead of moving something forward and creating value for which customers are willing to pay.

12. **Meeting** – without clear expectations of what must be different when you are done.

13. **Spinning** – creating deliverables and assignments to justify time and money expended. A favorite example is assignments dished out at the end of meetings. If you can dream up an assignment or two, people will feel better about all the time they spent in the meeting. Not! At least not for long. Not once they get back to their desks and realize their To-Do lists grew with tasks having little strategic value.

14. **Perfecting** – perfectionism is costly. Too often the last 20% adds zero value. If a tree falls in the forest and nobody is there to hear it, does it make a sound? Philosophers may still be debating that one, but here is a far easier one: If your finishing touches are discernible to no one but you, do they create value?

15. **Redoing** – because you didn't create the clarity of purpose and process that would have allowed doing it right the first time.

Clarity of Process

If you think these activities provide value, try adding them to the next customer invoice and see how eager your customers are to pay for them! Dismantle and replace them by insisting that all activities create value for which customers are willing to pay. Find that value or find a better way to spend your time.

Feeling Buried? Time to Regroup!

Employees at every level, from CEOs on down, tell me they are so caught up in daily details that they don't have time to step back and figure out where they are. They feel scattered, overwhelmed, and tired of running in high gear. Here is a quick method for reconsidering *what* goes on your To-Do list, followed by three tips for getting things *off* the list.

To Quickly Regroup:

Make a list of everything that is bothering you. Big things and little things. Don't think much, just write quickly.

Spend a little time with this mix of worries, plans, problems, and objectives. What is this list really telling you?

- Do you see things that are getting in the way of doing what you think you are supposed to be doing?
- Do you see things that are closely related, or problems that are the root cause of other problems?
- Do you see things that really aren't your concern?
- Do you see things that worry you but that you either can't fix or don't really need to fix?

With a little practice, the insights from this mix of items will help you quickly rethink the content of your To-Do list.

Now let's look at some tips to help you finish things and get them *off* your To-Do list. First, based on the list of questions, figure out what you can delete, delegate, and delay. Some tasks, if delayed sufficiently, can eventually be deleted. One trick is to spot those sooner and delete them so you can forget them. For the tasks that are undeniably yours, use the following three demarcations to match tasks with the attitude and support essential to successful resolution:

1. H is for Help

Some of the tasks on your list probably deserve to be marked with a big H: Help Needed. These are tasks for which you do not have enough information or expertise to handle efficiently and effectively.

These items are often at the core of your feelings of being overwhelmed. Even while working on something completely different, these are likely to be gnawing at the back of your mind. These tasks are also the ones that often hang out on your To-Do list the longest.

The H tells you that you need to find some help:

- clarity of purpose,
- better instruction,
- a specific method or plan of attack,
- advice,
- someone to bounce ideas around with,
- or more extensive help.

Until you get the information you need, you will be playing at the edges of these tasks rather than making real progress. It is much easier to identify the help you need than to solve the problem without help. And often, just trying to identify the help you need makes the problem clearer and points you to a solution.

2. B is for Block

Some tasks require time to concentrate without interruption. Mark these with a big B. In this day and age of multi-tasking, we are often interrupt-driven. Worse, we are so accustomed to being interrupted that we constantly interrupt ourselves.

To tackle the B problems:

- get them on your calendar,
- choose a time and place with fewer demands,
- give yourself a specific time period to work,
- turn off the email alert,
- forward the phone,
- hang out a do-not-disturb sign, and
- don't interrupt yourself until the time period expires or the task is complete.

3. D is for Discipline

These are the tasks you dread. Tackling them will be easier if you:

- tell yourself that prolonging the agony only makes the pain worse, and
- set a deadline and reward yourself once the task is complete, or,
- if all else fails, shame yourself into action: "Any self-respecting _____ would be embarrassed to admit this task is still undone a half hour from now!"

Now Make A To-Do Plan:

Rank tasks by importance, something you've undoubtedly done before. Be sure your sense of importance ties back to delighting customers, keeping the business strong, or supporting employees who are doing one of the former.

But you won't necessarily *do* the tasks in order of importance. The items marked Help, Block, and Discipline are not just going to suddenly happen when they rise to the top of your priority list. Use the Hs to get the help you need, the Bs to plan suitable blocks of time, and the Ds to set deadlines and rewards.

Is That Your Indecision Box?

You call it your inbox. A more accurate name might be your 'Indecision box.' Would you believe the average office worker spends 28% of working hours reading and writing email? If the 2012 McKinsey study[3] is still relevant, and I doubt things have improved, that's more than three months each work-year doing nothing but email! Imagine if your company could cut that time in half. What might your employees do with an extra six weeks each year? How many more customers could you serve with the same workforce? What would that do to employee stress levels, yours included?

How many times do you look at the same email message?

- Should I respond or not?
- How do I handle this?
- Should I sign up?
- If I ignore it, will it go away?
- Do I need to save this somewhere?

You know the questions. If you return to the same message multiple times, pondering those same questions, you are wasting time and energy. There are only four efficient responses to any email:

1. Act immediately (read or respond).
2. Save it for later (flagged by date or filed with relevant project).
3. Archive it (an overused option, but not ineffective).
4. Delete it.

---

[3] www.mckinsey.com/insights/high_tech_telecoms_internet/the_social_economy

Clarity of Process

To increase your success rate in making these choices, don't check email unless you have time to complete this process. If awaiting a particular message, check quickly and leave. Come back later when you have time to handle each appropriately in sequence. If your inbox isn't emptied a couple of times each day, you definitely have an Indecision Box instead! Worse than that, you have an E-mess! Do a spot check on employee inboxes and you'll know immediately which employees need help.

There is no reason to let email consume a quarter of your day. Here are five steps your company can take to reduce email immediately.

1. Don't tell people what they need to know.

Instead of telling people what they need to know, tell them what they need to do. And put that at the top of your message!

"I need your input on the Grafton proposal by 10:00 tomorrow. Contact Susan if you haven't received it. Let me know if you have questions."

If you absolutely must provide background information or advice, put that after the request. "You might want to keep in mind that..." or "Here is what has been agreed thus far..."

If your email doesn't leave the reader with a clear next step, your beautifully crafted message will:

- Be ignored and deleted.
- Or worse, clog an inbox.
- Or worse still, result in a flurry of additional emails.

You don't want to be the author in any of those situations.

2. Don't copy anyone unless you need something from them.

If you have thought through your needs as a result of #1, you shouldn't have anyone on the distribution list from whom you need nothing. Even silence should be seen as signifying agreement and support. No one receiving your message should be thinking, "This doesn't really apply to me."

3. Stop guessing.

Most email messages are overly complicated and time-consuming because the writer doesn't know what the reader knows or is thinking. So the writer guesses. Makes assumptions. Or spends precious time trying to anticipate every possible scenario. This is a huge waste of time for both the writer and the readers.

When we talk with someone, we get immediate feedback from our very first statement or question, and we adjust our next words accordingly. Imagine walking up to someone with a long scripted conversation and reading it without making any adjustments based on the reaction you receive. You'd look and sound like an idiot. But no more idiotic than your emails that go on and on without knowing what the other person is thinking.

If you can't reduce your email to a simple request (e.g., "I need your input on the Grafton proposal by 10:00 tomorrow"), pick up the phone or arrange a time to talk. You'll save a ton of time, avoid misunderstandings, and develop important cut-to-the-chase skills.

4. Don't use email if you can't expect crisp progress in response.

If your email is going to trigger a response more complicated than something like the following, don't use email. Here are the ideal responses:

- Done
- 2:00 Thursday
- Let's talk
- Yes

111

- No
- Thank you
- I recommend...
- I've decided...
- Only if...

The last thing you want to do is trigger a wandering or philosophical discussion over email.

5. Never use 'Reply All'.

Most email messages are sent to too many people to start with. "Reply All" doubles the wasted time. Do your colleagues a favor and leave them off the list.

Impress upon your organization the importance of these five rules and all of you will be spending much less time in your inbox!

4 Skills That Separate The Super Productive From Everyone Else

You have too much to do. Some days you feel productive, others leave you with too little to show for all of your time. Why can't you be one of those super productive people who chunks through tasks and goes home at 5:00pm?

You can if you practice four simple skills.

1. Choose

To join the ranks of the super productive, or even just the very productive, you have to know what you are trying to accomplish at any given moment. I'm not talking about major goals here, I'm talking about what will be different at the end of the next hour or quarter of an hour or even five minutes. What, specifically, is the next outcome you must achieve? How will you know when you are finished? Without clarity, you are wandering and, while it might be interesting, even fun, wandering is rarely productive. You don't want to just "work on something for awhile." Choose a specific destination and you will reach it faster.

The importance of Choosing does not depend on the type of task. Whether you are writing a proposal, running a meeting, or developing products, you will be most productive if you know exactly what success looks like each step of the way. What is the purpose of the proposal, what are the most important points, and which one are you working on right now? What decisions, plans, or problems will be resolved by your meeting and how will you get to each? What do you need from whom to get things moving?

While the main intent of Choosing is to allow you to focus on clear, specific, and immediate actions that represent real progress, the flip side of Choosing forces you to decide what you are not going to do. Multi-tasking is not effective. No matter how seamlessly you seem to be able to switch topics, you have only one brain and those transitions either reduce your depth of thinking or your speed. I remember when my first child was born. My brother was amazed that I could continue our conversation, even finish sentences many minutes after I started, despite repeated interruptions. Amazing? Maybe. But those conversations took all morning!

The first step to super productivity is to choose clear outcomes for every day, hour, quarter hour, and sometimes, even the next minute. Specificity creates clarity and clarity creates speed.

2. Start

Intentional starts are the second step to super productivity. "I am starting X right now and doing nothing but X for the next 30 minutes or until I finish."

You may think you do this, but more often than not, people don't start, they wander in. Perhaps you feel compelled to check for messages first. That's when you see a draft and decide to finish it quickly. Or you remember a phone call you need to return. Then you figure you may as well check Facebook too before diving into your task. When you open your browser, your default home page pops up with breaking news. Next thing you know, half an hour or more has slipped by and you still haven't started. Gee, maybe it's time to check your email once more before getting started!

Wandering in, by the way, is the only option whenever you don't consciously choose an endpoint. Without a clear next outcome, you are liable to start down two or three paths simultaneously. You may even devote a significant amount of time to 'doing stuff' before you realize it isn't what you need. This is busyness, not progress or productivity.

Conscious, intentional starts coupled with explicit, tangible next outcomes get you half the way to super productivity.

3. Focus

Once you know what you are trying to accomplish and have begun with clear intention, the next step is to focus! Keep at it until you are finished. To do this, you must prevent interruptions and distractions.

Close the door. Hang out a do-not-disturb sign. Forward your phone to voicemail. Turn off the sounds and notifications on your electronic devices. If you protect yourself from all distractions for 20, 30, 60, however many minutes you need, you will be amazed at what you can accomplish.

But you must also protect yourself from yourself! Clear the decks so you aren't distracted by other projects, half written emails, open documents, and notes stacked on your desk. Remove all of these from your peripheral vision and computer screen to eliminate distractions and maximize focus. If you need to check for an email relevant to your task, say out loud, "I need to see what Joe said in his last email and I will look at nothing else!" If you need to look up something on the web, do so with that same intentional focus. Don't wander into the web or your inbox with your guard down!

And don't interrupt yourself! Force yourself to forget about all texts, messages, and Facebook posts until you finish your task. People have become so accustomed to constant communication that they often interrupt themselves to check for communication. In many cases, this actually happens more often than being interrupted by others. Focus, focus, focus! Don't let yourself do anything else until the time expires or you reach the finish line of your task.

At first, you may find 20, 30, or 60 minutes an astoundingly long time to go without checking for messages. If so, you definitely need to practice focusing!

4. Finish

How often do you get most of the way there and decide to take a break, do something else, and finish the task later? Maybe you want to let your thoughts perk or clear your head or just eat lunch. Don't do it!

Choose, start, focus, and then *finish*! Really finish. Hit the send button. Print the document. Submit the request. Don't stop until you cross that finish line. Don't let yourself stop short and plan to review and finish later. Later you'll have to ramp up and get back into things. More often than not, that last review doubles the total time spent on the task while adding little value. No one but you is likely to appreciate the difference between the ultimate and penultimate outcomes. Unless the risk of failure is high or you are too emotional to think clearly, be done!

Choose, Start, Focus, Finish. Make this your mantra. Practice them religiously. These four skills are simple, but they are not easy. Choose, Start, Focus, Finish, and watch your productivity soar!

8 Tips That Will Turn 'Overwhelmed' Into 'Satisfied'

Work should be challenging and satisfying. It should fire you up to accomplish as much as you can and give you that great feeling of having made a difference. Unfortunately, those feelings are too rare. Too many people feel overwhelmed and overloaded. They leave work each day feeling they didn't accomplish enough. They suffer feelings of inadequacy and frustration. They question whether their employers are reasonable and fair. Some slip into victimhood, blame their employers, and abdicate responsibility for their own success and happiness.

Persistent feelings of inadequacy and unreasonable pressure are both destructive. They eat away at a person's confidence and determination. The goal should be to leave work each day feeling good about what you have accomplished and ready to make more progress the next day. There is simply no value in feeling overwhelmed or unhappy with your day at work.

One question I hear frequently is, "How do we know what constitutes reasonable goals?"

For the portion of your job that is predictable and repeatable and performed by several people (e.g., assembly line, processing paperwork, cleaning teeth), it is possible to measure performance, set standards, identify and disseminate best practices, and gradually increase the performance of everyone. For the portion of your job that is unpredictable and not repetitive, it is much harder to know how long things should take and what constitutes a successful day. So here are some tips that will make you more productive and make you feel more productive.

First off, at the end of each day, acknowledge what went well. Give yourself credit where credit is due. You'll probably never finish everything. Tomorrow is another day.

If you still feel bad, give yourself a break. For most of us, those unfinished tasks won't spark the end of the world as we know it.

Now let's look at what you can do if you didn't achieve as much as you thought you should have. You need to figure out why and decide what will make the next day more successful.

1. Were you clear about what you needed to achieve for the day overall as well as each hour or half hour or were you fishing without a concrete goal part of the time? Clear, concrete objectives are essential to speed. Don't wander in. Before you start any task, figure out what needs to be different when you are done and when you expect to finish. This is the first skill that separates the super productive from everyone else – Choose!

2. Were you following sound, step-by-step processes – tried and true methods – or were you muddling your way through? This is why we need greater Process Clarity. When you don't have a method, the first step is to figure out a method! Taking a moment to plan your approach instead of just diving in will save you time. If you perform any task frequently, you should constantly refine and improve your method to make it more efficient and effective. Work with your co-workers to generate ideas and cooperation where appropriate:

   - What are the essential steps?
   - What would success look like at each step?
   - How long should each step take?
   - What could we do to simplify and accelerate this work?
     - Would templates or checklists help?
     - Do I need greater clarity of purpose, process, or roles?

- Can we eliminate steps, cut corners that don't really matter, or find better resources in or outside our group or company?

3. Did you have the right tools, information, and other resources at hand when you needed them or did you waste time searching and waiting? If you lost time, figure out how to prevent a recurrence. This is especially important for familiar, repeatable tasks.

4. Were you focused and disciplined or did you let time slip away? The third skill that separates the super productive from everyone else is Focus. If you let time slip away, use the following steps to increase your focus and discipline tomorrow:

   - Know your priority at any given moment. Be sure it is a task that will make a difference.
   - Use my 'choose, start, focus and finish' technique to maximize your efficiency and discipline.
   - Use a timer and natural deadlines to keep time from slipping away.
   - Figure out how to reduce interruptions.
   - Enlist an accountability partner and/or make public commitments if deadlines motivate you.

5. Were you unavoidably and unexpectedly interrupted? If so, could it have been prevented? Are you booking your day too solidly to allow for inevitable interruptions? If you book every minute of your day, you won't be able to recover from any surprises

6. Do you believe you pretty much accomplished everything you could today? If yes, then quit beating yourself up and readjust your expectations. If not, why do you believe you could have accomplished more? (See steps 1-5.) Choose one new technique or action that will make tomorrow more successful.

- If you don't know where the day went, put a tablet on the side of your desk and use it to log your activity for the next several days. Figure out:
  - How often you are letting yourself get stuck, dwell too long, or get distracted.
  - How often you are being ruled by perfectionism, self-editing, consistency for the sake of consistency, self-interruption.
  - How often you are waiting for others.
  - How often you are wandering without clear goals and a process, etc.
  - Also, figure out what tasks just aren't up your alley and ought to be done by someone else.

7. Regardless of why you came up short, figure out how to deal with the work that didn't get or isn't getting done:

   - Get help. Outsource. Delegate.
   - Decide to work extra time (temporarily!).
   - Get rid of employees and customers who take up more time than they are worth.
   - Cut meetings in half and free up several hours a day.

8. Decide what will make tomorrow more successful. Practically everyone I know is on a journey to be more productive. It's epidemic. So here are a few final tips:

   - Keep in mind that you will be more productive if you smile, laugh, and give yourself downtime, sleep, exercise, and nutritious food.
   - Allow time periodically to examine your practices and seek better methods.
   - Give yourself time to learn and practice new skills.
   - Give yourself a break.

Now walk out that door, hold your head high, and smile. Tomorrow is another day and if you've been paying attention, you've got at least one idea that should make tomorrow a better day.

How to Minimize Effort and Maximize Results

We have been taught to be careful and thorough. We have been graded on accuracy. We are encouraged to be consistent. But being careful, thorough, accurate and consistent can be time consuming, counter-productive, and boring. There are only 24 hours in a day, and we have only one life to live. We will get better results and live better lives if we are careful, thorough, accurate and consistent where it counts, and speedy, efficient, and satisfactory everywhere else. "You can't be too careful," does not always apply.

Perfectionism is the first trap to avoid. I remember one of my mathematics professors at Tufts University deducting points from a perfect solution because a half-written, unused, abandoned formula off to the side was wrong. I prided myself on being right, armed myself with a big eraser, and my next exam was truly flawless. Perfect fuel for my perfectionism! Luckily, I eventually learned how unworthy and wasteful this characteristic was, and have gradually learned to squelch it. I wonder how many months of my life have been wasted trying to make unimportant things perfect. Perfectionism is notorious for driving up effort without improving results.

Consistency is another force with which we must reckon if we are to minimize effort and maximize results. Consistency can save time, improve collaboration, and make processes much more efficient. But consistency can also drive up the effort, causing you to do something just to be complete or because you always have. If you need an example from me of worthless consistency, your eyes must be closed.

A lack of clarity over objectives is the third most common and totally avoidable usurper of time. We leap to solutions before knowing what problem we are trying to solve. We argue about alternatives before we have agreed on what we are trying to accomplish. We create plans with great detail for the tasks we know and understand best, and gloss over the parts where we most need to focus. We control methods when we should be defining outcomes. We tell employees to work harder without clarifying goals and priorities. We satisfy urgency with activity, not the thoughtful pause that would help the most. Only with clear objectives is it possible to make a beeline to results achieved by following the most efficient path.

When tackling projects, wrangling over decisions, or admonishing your employees to do a good job, keep in mind that completeness, accuracy, consistency and activity should never be your goals. Define the desired outcomes instead. And then use good judgment to take every reasonable shortcut you can.

7 Secrets Smart People Know About Time Management

1. You can't manage time, you can only manage yourself.

There are 24 hours in each day. You can't change that. As long as you focus on managing time – searching for systems, lists, and tools – you are ignoring the real issue: how to manage yourself.

2. "Too much to do" and "Not enough time" are victim words.

Every time you repeat those words, you are letting yourself off the hook for managing yourself. You are blaming circumstances beyond your control and subscribing to victimhood. Of course there is too much to do! Of course there is not enough time! Get used to it!

3. Too many priorities means no priorities.

You cannot have too many priorities. By definition. Priorities are those top few tasks that deserve attention next. If you have too many, you have none. You have to know your top few priorities at any time.

4. The more priorities you have, the less you will accomplish.

The more items on your list, the more time you spend messing with the list, jumping from task to task, and feeling paralyzed by indecision. Take a look at the Abolish Priorities article if you don't believe me.

5. Your To-Do lists are crazy.

Pull all your lists together. Then try estimating the time needed to accomplish all of those tasks. What are the chances that the total exceeds all available time? Even if you shrink the numbers, convinced that you will suddenly be faster and more focused than ever, I bet the total exceeds the hours in a day.

6. Your To-Do lists are incomplete.

Not only are your lists crazy long, they are incomplete. Think about it. Have you included enough time for meetings, email, and phone calls? Questions from customers and staff? Time to sleep, eat, exercise, relax, and call your mother? What about time to search for everything from people to passwords? Or rebooting, correcting credit card expiration dates, and sitting on hold? Everything. Now how do those total hours look? And what are the chances you've anticipated everything likely to pop up? Face it, there are not enough hours in a day!

7. It's time to accept the fact that you won't finish everything.

As long as you believe you can – or need to! – finish everything, you will be frustrated and ineffective. And as long as you remain in denial, the longer you will avoid making the tough decisions about your top priorities.

When you fail to manage yourself, establish top priorities, and make conscious decisions about what to do and what not to do, the stress is unbelievable and the results aren't pretty:

- Squeaky wheels get the grease.
- Your inbox and meeting schedule control your day.
- Important tasks are trumped by easy tasks that you can dispense with quickly in exchange for the feeling of progress.
- *Fun* tasks, those for which you always have time and energy, somehow get finished.
- Short-term initiatives beat out long-term efforts.
- And every week you copy and sort those To-Do lists hoping they will magically become feasible.

It's time to bite the bullet, narrow your top priorities list to 2 – 3 items at any one time, schedule time on your calendar to tackle those items, and devote the rest of your energy to focusing and getting them done. Quit wasting so much time and energy listing, managing, and prioritizing the things that deserve to fall through the cracks.

The Worst Mistake You Can Make When Overloaded

When there is too much to do, things fall through the cracks, delays become epidemic, and stress spirals out of control. If others are involved, discord brews and respect erodes. The result is rarely pretty.

But it doesn't have to be that way. When there is too much to do, there are *only six possibilities*. The good news is that five of them are effective. The bad news is that most people choose the sixth!

Here are the five effective ways of dealing with overload:

1. **Accomplish more** – This option is simply wishful thinking unless you actually find a new, faster method that makes a measurable difference. You won't save significant time just trying to be faster and more disciplined.
2. **Postpone** – Some things can wait. Push them out.
3. **Cut corners** – Cutting corners sounds bad, but it isn't. Not everything has to be awesome or perfect. As a recovering perfectionist and software engineer, I know of what I speak! Just because engineers can create products with awesome features, doesn't mean the customer appreciates those features enough to foot the bill! Before starting any task, always ask the question, "How well?" Those last tweaks are usually discernible to no one but yourself.

4. **Ignore** – Some tasks just don't need to be done. Our lists fill up with them thanks to forces such as: consistency for the sake of consistency, old habits, business-as-usual, compulsiveness, favorite activities, bad processes, and unlimited cool ideas.

5. **Delegate or outsource** – Too many people are doing tasks that should never be on their plates in the first place. If you don't know how to delegate effectively and confidently, you need a dose of process clarity. If you are a control freak or simply unwilling to let go, knock it off!

What is #6?

The sixth choice, the only *ineffective* option, is to not consciously select one of the other five. Every one of the five is a valid option that can be managed for good results. But too often, people choose #6 by not deciding. And by not making the tough decision, they are leaving this decision to chance. The wrong things will fall through the cracks. The wrong corners will be cut. Whim, luck, and personal interests take control. The easy will triumph over the difficult, the tactical over the strategic, and the urgent over the important.

What will help me accomplish more?

One of the most common questions clients ask me, no matter the project, involves personal productivity. How do you know if someone could accomplish more? The answer is simple. They can.

But they won't automatically accomplish more just because you pile more on or ramp up the pressure! Nor will you accomplish more under those conditions.

Whether you are trying to accomplish more or you want your employees to accomplish more, here are some tips:

Clarity of Process

1. Be clear about objectives – Where are you leaping to solutions without finding root cause? When are you talking without an endpoint in mind? Are you getting important results or just staying busy?
2. Provide/get feedback – We often need external input to see the opportunities for improvement. How am I doing? Is there a faster method? Where am I wasting time?
3. Take a time out – Reflect on your own process, picture yourself doing your work, and track your own time. It is easy to get so caught up in the daily grind that we don't see opportunities to accomplish more.
4. Change your approach to tasks that slow you down – Where are the decisions you are slow to make, the times when you hesitate, when you overthink the situation, when you are reluctant to pull the trigger, the activities that always look like mountains? Find out what is really slowing you down. Break big objectives into concrete, bite size next steps.
5. Reconsider the things you enjoy doing – Where does that enjoyment lead to perfection, unnecessary enhancements, and puttering?
6. Find the tasks that should be easier – Where are you reinventing the wheel where a recipe, template, or standard procedure could make the task a snap?
7. Check your focus – Are you distracting yourself or letting others distract you unnecessarily?
8. Don't over plan – Planning is an important tool, but not an outcome. When perfect plans become the objective themselves, they cross the line into fiction, give the illusion of control, suck up vast amounts of time, and provide little actual value. Plan the familiar just enough to manage the interdependencies and plan the unfamiliar with the focus on learning and removing barriers as soon as possible. Go back and read the paper, *DRAW Your Plans* if you need more help.

What should I be delegating or outsourcing?

Individuals and organizations of all types are often slow to delegate or outsource. In many cases, it's a case of being penny-wise and pound-foolish. In other cases, it is simply the result of not taking the time to think through the possibilities, implications, and trustworthy alternatives. To get you started, identify activities that:

- Drain energy, things that simply aren't a good fit for the current resource.
- Are peripheral to your main focus and capabilities.
- Are performed infrequently, and therefore, probably inefficiently and ineffectively.
- Mastering will not increase your value to your customers.
- Are preventing you from doing the things that only you can do or that you must do well.

Isn't cutting corners bad?

'Cutting corners' has a reputation it doesn't deserve. Shoddy need not be the result. 'Good enough' really might be good enough. "If it's worth doing, it's worth doing well," is simply not good business thinking. Cutting corners is about making conscious decisions about how much time something deserves and how well it must be done.

Obviously, you must meet customer expectations. But, don't gold-plate your products. Engineers, for example, are notorious for providing cool features the customers don't care about. Craftsmen love polishing to perfection. Some people will rewrite documents and emails until the cows come home. In many cases, 80% is good enough. That extra 20% is usually visible only to you.

Before you start your next task, make a conscious decision about how well it must be done and how much time and effort it deserves.

Clarity of Process

How do I decide what to postpone?

The perennial winners in the fight over time are usually the urgent, the customers, and the squeaky wheels. But urgent does not mean important, customers are not all created equal, and squeaky wheels do not have to be fixed.

Here is where priorities are critical. And if you have too many priorities, you simply don't have priorities. *Abolish Your Priorities*, re-read the paper if you're not sure why! Then decide:

- What accomplishments would have the most positive impact on your future?
- If you can complete only three things, what must those be?
- Which customers are most important?
- What is urgent but not important?

What should I abandon?

Priorities are critical, but here are the two most important questions to consider:

- What are you doing that provides little return on investment now and/or in the future?
- What are you doing that contributes least to outcomes for which customers are willing to pay?

The former may send you back to your strategic drawing board. The latter may be as simple as:

- Are you reading and responding to emails that should just be deleted?
- Are you filing or saving things for later that you will never get to?
- Are you getting those unimportant ducks in a row before starting important tasks?

Choosing among the five effective methods for managing overload is not always easy, but that is what management is all about, whether we are talking about managing others or managing ourselves. Not making the decision, not choosing one of the five, is both risky and stressful.

3 Staggeringly Simple Steps To Accomplishing More Faster

In the previous article I explained that there are five effective ways to deal with having too much to do and one of those is to accomplish more faster. People try to do this all the time. They buckle down. They shut out distractions. And then they beat themselves up for failing.

Why do they fail? Because they aren't really doing anything differently. You know the old adage about the definition of insanity: doing the same thing over and over again while expecting different results. By that definition, most people are nuts. Every week, every day, they do essentially the same things and hope that somehow they will get caught up.

On top of that, people are faced with endless advice ranging from little tips to vast programs like Lean. Most people do not have time to digest all that they read or invest heavily in a process like Lean. So here's a simple way to reconsider your work and find a shorter, faster path. No new vocabulary or special tools are required. You can get as fancy as you like – but do that later. To get started immediately, embrace these staggeringly simple steps to accomplishing more:

1. Eliminate unnecessary work.
2. Eliminate unnecessary decisions.
3. Support necessary decisions.

Let's look at those one at a time.

1. Eliminate unnecessary work

As you walk through each activity of your day, ask yourself whether you would be proud to turn to a customer and say, "Isn't this great? This is what you are paying for!" Imagine saying this while digging through your inbox or sitting in endless meetings. Imagine proudly demonstrating your firefighting skills. Imagine explaining why you are still waiting for approval or feedback or any other information. Imagine defending the employee who has never been worth the trouble and should have been let go long ago. Picture that customer watching you reorganize and shuffle offices. Again. Or arguing at length about the wording of your mission statement, laboring over HR forms, or developing and attending internally focused programs so far removed from value creation that they are nothing more than chest-thumping pep fests. It's hard to stop listing examples because there are so many, but I recommend you take a walk through your own day as an imaginary tour guide to a customer.

Every example that makes you cringe with embarrassment at the thought of a watching customer is an indication that you are doing work that should be eliminated.

You want improvement? The first rule is to eliminate unnecessary work.

Identify it and take action. Everything you do should add value for which customers will gladly pay. There are a finite number of actions that move anything from an initial state to value for which customers are willing to pay. Any activity that isn't on the shortest path between those two points deserves scrutiny.

2. Eliminate unnecessary decisions.

Want to save time? Eliminate unnecessary decisions. Want to prevent mistakes? Eliminate unnecessary decisions. Want to reduce stress and friction? Eliminate unnecessary decisions. We make thousands of decisions each day. Each one is an opportunity for delay, mistakes, disagreement, and aggravation. Thus, rule #2 for better, faster results is to eliminate unnecessary decisions.

How do you eliminate decisions? You make them once and reuse them! You standardize your work. Wherever possible, you establish routines, templates, checklists, procedures, standard operating practices – anything that captures best practices, or even good-enough-for-now practices. When you standardize, you capture decisions so they don't have to be made over and over again. And you free up your brain and time for more important things.

3. Support necessary decisions.

You can't eliminate all decisions, obviously. But you want necessary decisions to be made quickly and effectively. By everyone in the organization! You want people to have the right competencies, inputs, decision guidelines, access to experts, tools, equipment, and authority to make smart decisions quickly. This is true whether employees are working individually or in groups.

How do you do this? First and foremost, you start paying more attention to decisions. Ferret out necessary decisions, understand the context in which they are being made, and then create a context that supports those decisions effectively and efficiently. Where do they occur in the standardized work? Who needs to make them? What inputs, rules, and guidance do those people need? What authority do they need? What structure and accountability systems will ensure they don't get bogged down?

I write frequently about the need for process clarity, especially shared process clarity and shared cognitive process clarity. My goal is to bring greater attention to process. Process clarity replaces willy-nilly physical and mental action with focus and sequence. It standardizes some aspect of the work. Here my goal is to bring greater attention to decisions. Decisions are the forks in the road that can stymie forward progress of any process, whether on the assembly line, when working with others, or sitting alone at your desk. Go back and re-read the section on *Clarity For Decisions*.

Eliminate unnecessary work, eliminate unnecessary decisions, and support necessary decisions. Those are the three simple steps to accomplishing more, faster.

Clarity Quiz – 21 Games People Play With To-Do Lists

If your To-Do list has more than three items, you are in trouble. Why? Because as soon as your list exceeds three items, it actually decreases your productivity. Most people have dozens of tasks on their lists and looking at those lists leaves them feeling exhausted before they even begin. In the face of these long lists, here are 21 games people play to feel more productive and/or less overwhelmed. All of these activities consume time and none of them help you accomplish more faster. Which ones do you play? Tick off the ones you play and add up your score to see how well you did.

1. Fill your To-Do list with tasks already completed.
2. Sub-divide existing tasks so you can check off the part you have finished.
3. List every little detail of new tasks so you can check more things off faster.
4. Copy the list to a clean sheet of paper.
5. Combine all your lists into one list.

6. Separate your list into multiple lists grouped by type of activity (e.g., phone calls, quick tasks, major tasks, morning tasks, between-meetings tasks).
7. Plot your tasks on a double axis chart with two axes: importance and urgency.
8. Mark each task with H, M or L.
9. Number the tasks in order of priority.
10. Re-number the tasks.
11. Devise a better scheme for prioritizing tasks.
12. Move the paper list to an electronic tool.
13. Move the electronic list back to paper.
14. Make a request of someone so you can move a task from your active list to your waiting-for-reply list.
15. Schedule a meeting to talk about tasks on your list so you don't have to worry about doing them in the meantime.
16. Forward a few emails to shorten today's list further.
17. List activities, not outcomes, so you can check things off without actually finishing anything.
18. Read the list in search of items you can finish quickly.
19. Read the list again to see if something else is more appealing or appropriate for your mood.
20. Read the list yet again to reassess priority.
21. Check the list one more time to see if you could possibly cross something else out.

Seriously now, what part of your day is devoted to managing or looking at your list versus getting something done?

If you scored less than 5, you are a To-Do List ninja. Keep up the good work! Find a way to share your techniques with others. Anyone scoring more than 5 would love to learn your methods.

If you scored 5 – 12, get help! First off, I guarantee your To-Do list is too long. Start each day by reducing your list to three tangible outcomes. Use the techniques in these papers, *Feeling Buried? Time to Regroup!* and *4 Skills that Separate the Super Productive From Everyone Else*, to finish those three before tackling more.

If you scored more than 12, cut it out!

Stop playing games with your To-Do lists. Accept the immutable limitations of time and hone your capacity to ruthlessly select your top priorities and find the shortest path to results.

In Conclusion – How Do You Reduce Effort & Save Time?

Below are a few tips you can begin using today to reduce effort and save yourself time.

When making decisions:

- Be clear about objectives before you deliberate over alternatives. What criteria and limitations are important to the decision?
- Waste as little time as possible on unimportant decisions. If several alternatives are 'good enough,' involve few people and little time in making the decision.
- Make decisions once and be done. Precious time is lost revisiting decisions. If you find this happening, you either aren't clear about the objectives or you haven't thought through the risks.
- Indecision often festers over the least consequential decisions. Ask yourself, "What's the worst thing that could happen?" If it isn't very bad, get on with things.
- Support decisions with the resources and authority that will allow those decisions to be sound and quick. Don't make qualified people jump through approval hoops, and don't leave unqualified people agonizing over decisions that shouldn't be theirs to make.

When solving problems:

- Ask first whether the problem – the deviation from the expected or desired outcome – is important. There are lots of problems that just aren't worth solving.
- Avoid leaping to solutions before you have identified the cause. Time is wasted daily on 'solutions' to the wrong problems.
- Get to the true cause of the problem.
- Eliminate the cause, don't ameliorate the effect.
- Test drive your solutions before unleashing the fanfare or torturing too many people.

When establishing plans:

- Be clear about what you are trying to accomplish.
- Match the detail of your plans to the risk involved.
- Ask yourself what could go wrong.
- Consider the seriousness and likelihood of each potential problem.
- Devote your resources to the serious and the likely.

'Minimize effort and maximize results' is as worthy a mantra as any. Call it lazy, if you like. I prefer to think of it as bringing a laser focus, *Uncommon Clarity®*, on that which is important and avoiding everything else.

Clarity for Meetings

*"Unproductive meetings have nothing to do with meetings and
everything to do with a lack of clarity."*
Ann Latham

Don't start a meeting until you know what must be different when the meeting ends!

With what will you walk away?

What tangible outcomes will allow you and the other participants to move something forward a mile?

This is absolutely *the* most important lesson if you want short, powerful meetings.

Everyone Hates Meetings

Ask who loves meetings and you'll get no takers. I've never worked with any company where people don't complain about bad meetings. Meetings break up the day into unproductive slivers, bore people to death, drive unnecessary work, and rarely produce sufficient value to justify the cost of the resources sitting in the room or on the phone. People hate meetings. Meetings are evil.

Well, I've got bad news for you. Meetings aren't evil. Meetings are how we work together. Unless you are completely isolated and autonomous, which describes exactly no employee I've ever met, you need to work with others to do your job. When you work with others, you are meeting. You may not call it a meeting until there are at least three people working together, but it is still a meeting. If you suddenly are unable to make real progress when others are involved, the problem is that you don't know how to work together efficiently and effectively. Unfortunately, you are normal.

Of course, the problem probably isn't your meetings, right? Few people see their own meetings as unproductive. It is everyone else's meetings that are a problem. But that just proves my point. You and your colleagues have a lot to learn about how to work together efficiently and effectively. Unproductive meetings have nothing to do with meetings and everything to do with a lack of clarity. Stop blaming the meetings!

Should You Have a Meeting?

The first question to ask yourself, before setting an agenda, deciding who to invite, or booking the room, is: should we actually have a meeting? Before deciding, read these top mistakes and the reasons for and against scheduling a meeting.

Meeting Mistake #1: Not knowing what must be different when you are done

Never start a meeting without knowing specifically what must be different when you are done. What tangible progress will you walk away with? Which of *Latham's Six Outcomes* are you pursuing? Review the paper entitled *Want Results? Speak The Language Of Outcomes!* before you plan a meeting.

Meeting Mistake #2: Using Treadmill Verbs™

Bad meetings are unavoidable if *Treadmill Verbs*™ dominate your agenda and conversation. Remember that *Treadmill Verbs*™ are verbs without a destination. They invite endless talk, not outcomes.

Meeting Mistake #3: Debating how before what

Whether establishing plans, making decisions, or resolving problems, there seems to be an irresistible urge to discuss 'how' before determining 'what'.

- Generating ideas for how to implement before determining what needs to be achieved.
- Debating alternatives before establishing objectives when making a decision.
- Tossing out ideas for how to solve a problem before identifying the cause of the problem. Read *SPOT Remover for Problems*, again for ways to identify and eliminate your problems.

"What are we trying to accomplish?" is one question that will save enormous amounts of time and prevent you from debating the how before settling the what. Look at the papers on *SOARing Through Decisions*™, *DRAWing Your Plans*, and *SPOT Removing Problems* to ensure you establish clarity of purpose and process before leaping into any debate.

Meeting Mistake #4: False start

Another leading cause of ineffective time-wasting meetings is neglecting to establish a shared starting point.

To avoid this problem, begin by stating what has been completed or decided thus far and what you perceive as the next step. If there is agreement, you've just framed the conversation clearly. If there is disagreement, you've just saved the group from a jumbled, frustrating, and unproductive discussion. It doesn't matter whether you are making decisions, plans, or solving problems. Once again, review the papers on *SOARing Through Decisions™*, *DRAWing Your Plans*, and *SPOT Removing Problems* and use the first step of each to establish a shared starting point and agreed first step.

Seven poor reasons for having a meeting

I am sure there are more good reasons to call a meeting than poor reasons. However, I think I have been to more meetings that happened for poor reasons. These include:

1. We always meet on the 4th Tuesday of the month or first thing Monday mornings (meeting because it is time).
2. We haven't had a meeting in a long time (meeting because it is time).
3. The boss formed this team so I guess we better have a meeting (meeting because we were told to).
4. We need to tell people what is going on (meeting as a substitute for written communication).
5. We need a meeting to figure out what we should do at our meeting (meeting as an alternative to doing the homework of planning and/or analysis).
6. We need a meeting so people will feel they were heard and believe they had a say (meeting as manipulation).
7. We need to meet or this just won't get done (meeting as an alternative to self-discipline and accountability).

Note: This doesn't mean you shouldn't meet if the above are true, it just means these are not reasons in themselves for having a meeting.

Seven good reasons for having a meeting

Wondering when it makes sense to call a meeting? Here are some excellent reasons:

1. You need to leverage multiple perspectives and varied expertise in order to understand a situation or sequence of events, identify alternatives, make a decision, uncover risks, assess consequences, etc.
2. You need to quickly compare plans before everyone runs off in opposite directions as a means of clarifying priorities, communicating last minute changes, and minimizing resource conflicts.
3. You want everyone to have the opportunity to hear the same message, particularly when part of that message will be delivered through hard-to-predict Q&A.
4. It is important for everyone to hear the message at exactly the same time.
5. You need to build commitment to a decision or course of action through broad discussion.
6. You need to develop employee skill and awareness through discussion of priorities, issues, alternatives, and risks.
7. The accomplishments of a group deserve public recognition.

Time spent clarifying the purpose of a meeting is always time well-spent. In determining your purpose, it will be easier to work out the details if you think hard about the specific outcomes you desire. In general, people should leave with specific, tangible outcomes that represent progress and that did not exist before the meeting began.

But if you really want meetings to be effective, the first step is to acknowledge that meetings themselves are not evil. On the contrary, meetings are essential. How could they not be? If your meetings are bad, you must take responsibility for making them better, read on to find out how.

The Meeting Process

Following this advice can cut your meetings in half at the very least!

Before a Meeting Step #1: Only three reasons to meet

Before you even get started, you need to be sure a meeting is necessary.

There are only 3 reasons for having a meeting (virtual meetings included):

1. Reduce total time devoted to achieving a desired outcome.
2. Improve the quality of a desired outcome.
3. Build relationships.

If you don't expect to save time, improve the results, and/or build important relationships, don't call a meeting. Furthermore, if the outcomes are not worthy of this kind of investment of time and energy, don't call a meeting.

Before a Meeting Step #2: Latham's Six Outcomes – which are you pursuing?

Never start a meeting without knowing what must be different when the meeting ends. As we discussed in the introduction, you should always be working toward one of *Latham's Six Outcomes* during any meeting:

1. A decision.
2. A plan.
3. A problem resolution.
4. A list of ideas or inputs that contribute to one of the above.
5. Confirmation (Am I on the right track?)
6. Authorization (May I?)

Each of these is a recognizable, tangible outcome. You will know when you are done if you strive for any of these.

Before a Meeting Step #3: Only four reasons to include others – use these to identify participants

Whom should you invite to your meeting?

There are only four reasons to invite others to your meeting:

1. To improve the quality of the outcomes, invite people with relevant skills, knowledge, and experience.
2. To improve commitment to those outcomes, invite people who must execute, support, or approve necessary actions or people with the credibility to represent those important to execution.
3. To build relationships, invite people who need to interact well or better for success.
4. To provide an employee with a developmental opportunity.

Keep in mind that #3 and #4 are not reasons for holding a meeting! The best way to develop relationships is either to work together or play together. I remember one prospective client who wanted me to facilitate a retreat. As usual, I asked what he wanted to accomplish. Once it became clear that his primary objective was to build relationships, I told him to save his money and take the group to play paintball or go on a boat ride.

As for meetings as developmental opportunities, a well-run meeting can be enormously beneficial for non-contributors to learn about the organization's priorities and to develop business acumen. Two caveats: It must be a well-run meeting and don't use this as an excuse to invite everyone and his brother.

Given the caveats associated with #3 and #4, I will not refer to them again!

Of course, you can't answer questions about whom to invite unless you are clear about your desired outcomes.

Before a Meeting Step #4: "You! Call 911!" – prepare the participants

"You! Call 911!" produces far better results than "Help!" Set clear expectations to increase effectiveness and participation of invitees:

- Tell participants why they have been invited. See previous point – Only 4 Reasons to Include Others.
- Tell them specifically what kind of input you expect and whether preparation is expected. Provide the equivalent of "You! Call 911!"
- Tell them whom they are representing, if anyone.

Don't take these things for granted. Meeting participants may be trying to protect their direct reports from work overload while you believe they are representing the customer's best interests. They aren't at fault if that is the case, but they won't necessarily provide you with the perspective and insights you need either.

Setting these expectations also gives invitees the opportunity to suggest better-qualified resources.

Before a Meeting Step #5: Create an agenda

Define Outcomes:

- Crystal clear outcomes are essential!
- Don't even think of creating an agenda if you don't know what must be different when the meeting ends!
- Don't even think about using *Treadmill Verbs*^{TM}!

Define Intermediate Outcomes:

- The fastest path to your desired outcome is nothing more than a series of intermediate outcomes, each as tangible as the final desired outcome.
- An agenda is a roadmap of intermediate outcomes leading to the final desired outcomes.

Ask!

- Once you know what you want, ask for it!
- Your agenda should be a series of questions requesting each outcome, whether final or intermediate.

For more information about how to create a great agenda see the following paper: *97% Of Agendas Are Recipes For Wasting Time – Are Yours?*

Before a Meeting Step #6: Prepare to lead

What do you need to succeed? Figure it out and make it happen. Everyone is different. Possibilities include:

- Help identifying desired outcomes.
- Help identifying intermediate outcomes.
- Help converting your desired outcomes into specific questions.
- Help identifying resources needed to achieve your desired outcomes.
- Help recognizing when people are off track.

- Rough timeframes so you can maintain progress.
- Someone to watch the clock for you.
- A 'parking lot' for recording important but off topic ideas.
- Ground rules.
- Someone to keep *you* focused.
- Permission from the group to interrupt if they wander.
- The courage to assert yourself if they wander or you aren't sure the conversation is relevant.
- A plan for dealing with someone who dominates, derails, discourages, or disrespects.
- A sense of humor for reducing tension.
- A min/max plan so you aren't disappointed if you don't get as far as you had hoped.
- A facilitator so you can concentrate on content and not process.

Prepare to lead. Ask for help where you need it.

During a meeting:

- Come prepared with your agenda and input.
- Keep the group focused on achieving the desired outcomes.
- Confirm the achievement of each desired outcome as it occurs so all leave with the same understanding and sense of accomplishment.
- Stop the meeting if you don't have the right people or information to achieve your desired outcomes.
- Stop the meeting if you get lost and are no longer sure of either your desired outcomes or the intermediate outcomes that will get you there.
- Honor the scheduled end time. Tangible intermediate outcomes provide clear progress even if the final desired outcome is not realized.

If you begin the meeting with clear outcomes, specific intermediate outcomes where needed, and the right people in the room, running the meeting is the easy part.

After a meeting:

- Follow up on the official outcomes so the meeting's value isn't lost.
- Follow up on the 'parking lot' issues, those items that were raised but not addressed, so people trust the 'parking lot' and are willing to let go of important issues in favor of the meeting priorities.
- Reflect on the effectiveness and efficiency of the meeting.
- Review 'Before the Meeting' pointers.
- Determine how your next meeting can be more powerful still.

Verify Outcomes

Are you achieving your objectives? Are people leaving the meeting with a common understanding of purpose, perspective, decisions and/or action items? The best way to find out is to ask.

At the end of a meeting, ask each participant to take three minutes to write down the main outcomes as they see them. Obviously, it is important to stress that the purpose is to improve meetings, but your individual situation will determine how much care is needed to keep this from being too threatening. No names are needed, and a neutral individual can collect and summarize the comments and then report back to the group or the leader. You might be surprised to discover that the three main points that you thought were crystal clear aren't even mentioned.

The benefits of this quick assessment include:

1. Participants will become more alert.
2. Participants will start asking for more clarity.
3. You will get better at providing the focus needed.

Meeting Evaluation Criteria

Clarity of objectives.

Selection of participants.

Preparation and participation of participants.

Respect and teamwork.

Clarity of process.

Process discipline.

Clarity of outcomes.

Value of outcomes.

Reality check (data driven decisions, realistic expectations).

Good use of time.

97% Of Agendas Are Recipes For Wasting Time – Are Yours?

Agendas are king. This message has been pounded into us long enough to be well-ingrained, even if not always followed. But have you noticed that despite the proliferation of agendas, everyone is still complaining about meetings? That's because 97% of agendas are simply recipes for wasting time.

8:00 – 8:15 Waste time on this

8:15 – 8:30 Waste time on that

8:30 – 8:50 Waste more time

Before I dive in, why don't you grab a few agendas so you can see what I am talking about.

First off, you need to keep in mind that the purpose of any meeting is to get somewhere. To make something happen. And you won't get anywhere if you don't know where you are trying to go. You have to have a destination. You have to know what must be different when the meeting ends.

Clarity of Process

This may seem obvious, but it's not. People who know I deplore unproductive meetings have been known to tell me about great meetings. When I ask them what made the meeting great, I typically get three reasons:

1. The group was focused.
2. The topic was interesting.
3. Everyone was well-behaved.

That's it! There is no mention of outcomes! Just because you had an interesting discussion does not mean your meeting was productive.

Now back to those agendas. Most agendas waste time because they are filled with those dreaded *Treadmill Verbs*™. Now the good news is that while there are an unlimited number of *Treadmill Verbs*™ and nouns you could put on an agenda, there are only six *Destination Verbs* that lead to *Latham's Six Outcomes* and discernible progress. Use these and they will transform your meetings:

1. Decide.
2. Plan.
3. Resolve.
4. List.
5. Confirm.
6. Authorize.

These six are all you need, and they all demand a destination. If your destination is a decision, you will know you are done as soon as you make that decision. If your destination is a list, whether a list of actions, resources, or risks, you will know you are done as soon as you have your list. Do you need confirmation that you are on the right track? You will know you are done as soon as you hear, "Yup, keep going." Do you need authorization to proceed? You will know you are done as soon as you hear a yes, no, or first we need to resolve, plan, decide, list, or confirm something else.

There is no room for discussing, reviewing, reporting, and updating in our crazy busy world. Get those *Treadmill Verbs™* and nouns off your agendas! If you can't specify your destination, you need help. Do not start a meeting without knowing what must be different when the meeting ends!

5 Reasons Meetings Never Improve

Unless you've had your head in the sand or like to waste time, you know meetings suck up a tremendous amount of valuable time. You've also read lots of advice that is supposed to help. You've probably even tried some of that advice. And you are not alone.

So why is it that meetings are still wasting so much time and everyone is still complaining about them?

This is why: 99% of the advice you've heard for improving meetings doesn't work.

1. Typical advice assumes meetings are the problem.

It's as if meetings create some sort of evil force that destroys time and renders people incompetent. To conquer that force, we need rules and tools to control people.

But meetings are not the problem. Meetings are just how we work together. Unproductive meetings have nothing to do with meetings and everything to do with a lack of clarity. Meetings simply expose and amplify any lack of clarity. If you are unclear about what you are trying to accomplish while sitting alone at your desk, no one need know. You might not even recognize the fact yourself. But walk into a room full of people and let all the horses out of the barn, and it's just luck if anything is accomplished. As a matter of fact, the more helpful, determined, intelligent, and extroverted the group, the more different and interesting directions they can take any topic!

149

2. Typical advice focuses on tools.

Tools like agendas top most lists. But most agendas actually increase waste because you not only waste time in the meeting, you waste time creating the agenda, especially if you take the time to get the formatting right. The vast majority of agendas simply prescribe how you are going to waste the time and do nothing to prevent the waste of time. Every day I witness serious, earnest people talking about agenda topics with great discipline. Unfortunately, just because a discussion is focused, disciplined, and interesting, doesn't mean anything is accomplished.

Time frames are another favorite tool. By assigning limited time, the hope is that somehow, something will be accomplished. If nothing else, you can let the clock decide you are done so you lose less time. This advice is usually coupled with suggestions about big clocks or an hourglass. Dripping sand can pump up the pressure and make people talk faster, but it will not improve their ability to make group decisions.

3. Typical advice creates rules to control people.

One favorite rule is locking doors at the starting time. Since when does it make sense to continue without critical voices present? You wouldn't invite anyone to a meeting who wasn't critical, would you? Maybe if meetings were productive and participants were critical, people would arrive on time! If not, I suggest you tell them how rude they are.

Another rule is to forbid speaking until a ball or some other object is passed to you. This is supposed to ensure only one person talks at a time. (It is especially effective in the winter. "Please pass the germs!") If your employees don't know how to take turns talking, they need the course on civil behavior, not on effective meetings.

Here is one more ineffective rule: Leave cell phones at the door. If your meetings are really effective, everyone will forget about their cell phones. No one will be texting or checking email. The only interruptions will be the right interruptions – emergencies.

No chairs. Another favorite of mine. Standing may make people uncomfortable and eager to be done, but since when does pain improve decision making?

4. Typical advice prescribes roles.

Roles are another misguided effort to improve meetings. I always feel sorry for these people. The minute taker dutifully records, but how does that increase the likelihood of results? If you actually make a list or a decision, it certainly makes sense to write it down, but taking notes will do nothing to ensure that happens.

Time keepers are equally helpless. They get to watch time fly and try to interrupt, but mostly they just get to be the person most painfully aware every minute the group spends making little progress.

5. Typical advice does nothing to address the root cause of ineffective meetings.

Meetings are effective only if you walk out with specific results that you didn't have going in. And that will only happen quickly and effectively if you walk in knowing what needs to be different when the meeting ends. What decision or list or plan, specifically, do you have to have in your hands at the end to move things forward? If you aren't clear about this, you will do what just about everyone does. You will review, report, discuss, communicate, and update – all *Treadmill Verbs*™ with no destination. No way to know when you are done. No way to know which direction to go. Or maybe you will try to do nouns. Check out all those agendas everyone insists on these days. See any *Treadmill Verbs*™ or nouns? How can you possibly know when you are done when you get on one of those treadmills?

The root cause of poor meetings is a lack of clarity. None of the typical advice teaches you how to create clarity. If you want to accomplish twice as much in half the time, you must have:

1. **Clarity of purpose** – What, specifically, must be different when the meeting ends?
2. **Clarity of process** – What series of intermediate outcomes will get you to your final outcome?

Use *Latham's Six Outcomes* to keep you focused on progress. If you don't know which you are pursuing, you are unlikely to get there. For more on these six outcomes, read the introduction – *Want Results? Speak the Language of Outcomes!* Specificity creates clarity and clarity is the secret to short and powerful meetings.

The Worst Way to Open a Meeting is Probably One You Use

"Do you want to start or should I?"

This is the worst possible way to open a meeting. And, yet, it is also among the most common. Epidemic, actually. I think it must be contagious.

Why is it bad?

Because it opens the door wide. It's an invitation to talk. It lets the horses out of the barn. Anyone with a topic that seems relevant to the group, whether a beef or a great idea, can take advantage of the vacuum to make a suggestion. Even if you address the question to a specific person, it doesn't prevent others from chiming in while they have the chance.

Secondly, it's an abdication of responsibility. And it reduces your credibility. Diminishes your leadership stature. If you are running the meeting, you are supposed to know who needs to start.

Third, it sets an overly democratic tone for the direction of the meeting. And that scares everyone. When busy people show up, they don't want a free-for-all. They want someone with a plan who will cut to the chase and accomplish something.

So why do you do it?

"Do you want to start or should I?" is a self-conscious gesture caused by one of five situations:

1. You don't have a clear idea of what you are trying to accomplish.
2. You don't have a clear process for achieving what you want to accomplish.
3. You don't have a clear idea of the roles people must play in order to achieve your objective.
4. You know what you want from others, but haven't told them.
5. You are just trying to be polite. You're a nice, caring, collaborative person! And you don't realize that you are letting the horses out of the barn.

If you don't know what you are trying to accomplish, shame on you! There is no excuse for that. That is completely irresponsible and disrespectful of people's time. You should never start a meeting without knowing what must be different when it ends. Review *Want Results? Speak the Language of Outcomes!* In the Introduction.

If you have a clear outcome in mind, but haven't thought through the process that will get you to those tangible outcomes, shame on you once again! Ambling and rambling is not a productive use of time. How dare you assemble all these people without a clear process!

Thinking through the roles people must play is quite intricately tied up with thinking through the process. Albeit, another level of detail. But this isn't difficult. Generally speaking, you either need their input to make smart decisions or you need their cooperation to implement. Sometimes you need both. But there is no excuse for not knowing what you need from each person you invited and whether what they have to say should come first!

Why You Should Outlaw Informational Meetings

I tell my clients they must put an end to informing each other.

Why?

Because *inform* is a *Treadmill Verb*™. And like other *Treadmill Verbs*™, such as report and review, it has no destination. There is no way to know when you are done. It is an open invitation to talk on and on with no particular outcome in mind. It leaves people listening, assuming they are listening at all, for nothing in particular. Thus, it accomplishes little, encourages smart phone tinkering, and leaves most people bored and disengaged.

Unfortunately, inform remains a favorite agenda item. Even die-hard fans of mine who have memorized *Latham's Six Outcomes* still argue that it is important to simply inform people.

So let me offer some alternatives that are much more productive. Let's replace those treadmill discussions with destination-oriented approaches. In doing so, we will dramatically shorten the conversation, increase engagement, and improve results.

The most common use of inform is to explain efforts-to-date and plans for next steps. Thus, you begin with, "This is what I've done and this is my plan." Right? But tell me, what do you really need? And why should they care?

Once you know the answer to those questions, you have a destination – a purpose. That destination will make it easier to provide the right background information. It will also make it easier to get what you need.

Here are six substitutes for inform that will make people sit up and take notice. Each begins with "Here is my plan." [Note: *Latham's Six Outcomes* are shown in italics in these examples.]

1. Here is my *plan*. Am I messing with your *plan*? Does either your *plan* or mine need to change?
2. What am I missing? I need a *list* of missing tasks or resources.
3. What could go wrong? I need a *list* of potential problems that I should consider.
4. Am I on the right track? I need *confirmation* before I continue.
5. May I proceed? I need *authorization* so I can continue.
6. I cannot succeed without your cooperation. I need *confirmation* that you can support my plan.

I don't care if you are using email or a meeting to inform, I guarantee that you will accomplish far more if you replace your treadmill informing with one or more of these outcome-oriented approaches. If you aren't pursuing one of *Latham's Six Outcomes*, you're just talking.

One Proven Technique You Can Use Today To Finish Work Early

I tried to keep quiet. Honest! This executive team did not know me yet, and I wanted to get off on the right foot. So I listened patiently, waiting for my appearance in their agenda.

Until I could stand it no longer. That's when I interrupted.

The team was smart, serious, earnest, and focused. But they weren't clear. They didn't have a clear purpose or process. As a result, they were talking intelligently, but going nowhere fast. In just the first five minutes, I had identified five decisions and two plans – seven different threads – under discussion.

They were a bit taken aback when I interrupted. They were indignant when I told them why. But as soon as I itemized the seven threads, they knew I was dead on. On top of that, they were instantly energized. It was as if I had opened the starting gates and turned them loose on a straight track to a finish line that had just become visible in the fog. The clarity I created with my itemized list reduced a complex mess that they could have talked about for hours to seven distinct tasks. And the order in which those tasks needed to be achieved was obvious. The team quickly dispensed with each one, one at a time, in synch with each other like never before.

Fifteen minutes later, those decisions and plans were in place and the executives were ready to move on. Had I not interrupted, my experience tells me the conversation would have circled for another half hour, or however long the leader thought they could allow, nothing would have been decided, and another meeting would have been scheduled.

While multi-threaded conversations are normal, they are not efficient and effective. They waste time, cause frustration, lead to decisions by exhaustion instead of intelligence, and erode profits.

So how do you prevent multi-threaded conversations that make progress next to impossible? The first step is to recognize them. The next time you attend a meeting, try counting the number of different threads under discussion.

The second step is to pause before you jump into a discussion and determine as specifically as possible what you are trying to accomplish. The key to clarity and focus is specificity.

If that is difficult for you, brainstorm a list of questions that must be answered to intelligently address the topic under consideration. Your list might look completely random, but that's OK. Once you have a list, the appropriate order of those questions is usually quite obvious and the unnecessary tangents are easily crossed off. Now you focus on one issue at a time. If you are working with others, this technique will get you on the same page and pool your expertise and brain-power. This is what I did for the executive team mentioned at the beginning of this article. This is what you need to do for yourself and your teams before the horses escape from the barn and start chasing a multitude of interesting, related, but utterly distinct conversations.

Clarity Quiz – What One Factor is Most Essential to Great Meetings?

Which of the following is most essential to an effective meeting?

1. An agenda.
2. On time start and finish.
3. Assigned roles (e.g., time keeper).
4. Ground rules (e.g., cell phones off).
5. Assigned action items.
6. Knowing what needs to be different when the meeting ends.

If you selected number 6, you are correct!

In Conclusion – Something Must Be Different When You Are Done

If you are looking for permission to cancel a meeting because you don't know what will be different when you are done, consider it granted!

Establishing and communicating clear, tangible outcomes for the meeting is absolutely your first priority. Getting others involved in helping you make it a success is the second.

When a meeting is successful, everyone leaves with a shared understanding of the specific tangible outcomes that did not exist when the meeting began.

PART THREE:
CLARITY OF ROLES

*"If you try to do something **to** another you will likely fail.*
*If you try to do something **with** another you can accomplish far more."*
Ann Latham

Why You Need Greater Clarity of Roles

Nothing is accomplished unless individuals take action. But not just any action. Random action inspired by individual hopes and desires creates chaos, not strategic results. Efforts must be made to align individual actions behind strategic priorities. People need to know quite specifically what must be done and by when.

If you want employees to be able to exercise good judgment and make smart decisions, they also need to know why things are being done and being done in certain ways.

If you want efficiency in addition to good results, people also need to know how, how well, and with whom they must work to achieve the desired results.

Now you could just tell everyone what to do. But that won't work. For two reasons: one, you don't have all the answers and two, people are not machines.

No, top down efforts to control people can't cover all the bases, nor garner the commitment you need to overcome obstacles. Thus, to align employees behind your strategic priorities and ensure they work effectively together, you need:

1. To help employees understand the challenges and priorities of the organization so they can make smart decisions about what must be done, when, how, how well, and with whom.
2. To encourage employee commitment, effectiveness, and productivity by empowering them with respect, authority, knowledge, self-awareness, credit, and feedback.

If you succeed, your employees will be able to create the day-to-day clarity of roles essential to effective collaboration and success.

Clarity for Leadership

"Whoever coined the term 'leadership style' did the world a disservice. Leaders with a specific style fail when a different style is needed."
Ann Latham

Remember that leadership isn't about the leader. Whoever coined the term 'leadership style' did the world a disservice. No matter what 'style' you consider to be yours, from autocratic to consensus-driven, you will be effective only in those situations where that approach makes sense and ineffective in all other situations. Good leaders adapt. They establish a clear direction and generate enthusiasm and commitment in others regardless of the situation.

Top Leadership Mistakes

If I had to pick the top leadership mistakes of executives from all the leaders I've encountered as a consultant and as an employee, they would be arrogance and confusing consensus with commitment.

Leadership Mistake #1: Arrogance

You are not the smartest person in the room. And even if you are, it is irrelevant. You cannot do every job in the company by yourself. You do not know best about the world in which your employees struggle and succeed daily. You are not solving a puzzle in a cave. You are leading humans. Without whom you cannot succeed. Treat them all with respect. They are your partners.

Leadership Mistake #2: Confusing consensus with commitment

You can gain commitment without gaining consensus and consensus without gaining commitment. Confusing the two wastes precious time and energy. Commitment is the goal, not consensus.

Seeing-Eye Boss

You tell them over and over again, but they don't seem to get it. They don't get it, so you don't trust them. You don't trust them, so you don't give them more responsibility. You have to do things yourself. Plus, you have to keep them under control. How will you ever make real progress?

You won't. Not alone. You need their help. All of them. But first, they need your help.

Read the first sentence of this article again. See how much trouble is caused just because they don't seem to get it? But that isn't the root cause – their inability to get it. It all starts with the telling. Have you really done what you can to help them understand what you are trying to tell them?

An employee with a clear understanding of your strategy, priorities, plans, and the associated challenges and risks, is worth far more than an employee doing his job without that understanding. An aware employee can contribute to the company's success not only by staying focused and using good judgment, but by seeing things you don't see, hearing things you don't hear, thinking of ideas you wouldn't think of, anticipating problems you can't anticipate, supporting others when you aren't present – the list goes on and on. You can't do it all, know it all, or be everywhere. You need aware employees.

But employees need your help to achieve this awareness. Helping your employees understand your strategy, priorities, risks and plans requires regular, ongoing dialog. Their attitudes, skill, experience and existing knowledge will affect what they hear in ways that you cannot possibly imagine. The only way to know if your communication efforts are succeeding, is to listen. And listening is easier if you ask good, open ended questions. Adapt the following questions to your situation:

- How will this affect our customers?
- How will this affect the people in your group?
- What can you do to help your people understand?
- What makes this hard?
- What skills might we need to develop?
- What attitudes and behaviors will it be important to encourage?
- What resistance should we expect?
- What resources might you need?
- What will you do differently tomorrow?
- How does this affect other priorities?
- Who else needs to be involved?
- What will you have to do to make this successful?

Whether following up on a discussion about a new situation or keeping tabs on a situation underway for many months, open-ended questions such as these will give you the opportunity to see how your employees are thinking about their work, their problems, their people, and more. Meet one on one with employees regularly. Listen respectfully and carefully. Guide them gently as a teacher might. Help their understanding grow along with their confidence.

Keep in mind that the world looks very different from their position. To think like you, they would have to have lived your life. To see the workplace as you do, they would have to have your job. To understand exactly what you say, they would have to share your brain. And to communicate honestly with you, they have to trust you. Telling is not communication. Ask sincerely, listen carefully, and respond from the perspective that it is you who is still missing something, not the employee. When you finally see what they see, they will see what they didn't see.

Captain of Your Own Ship

Whether you are the CEO or the last bottle washer, you will perform your best and be happiest if you are captain of your own ship! Master of your fate! This is true for everyone, at every level of your company.

Granted, some people's ships are bigger than others but in every case, we are all at our best – proudest, most motivated, happiest, and most successful – when captain of our own ship, when we know what we are about and can control our own fate.

But you can't be captain if you don't know you have 'a ship' and understand what constitutes 'your ship.' And you don't want to be an organization of pirates, even well intentioned pirates, who commandeer ships on whim.

Help each of your employees set sail with confidence by working with them to clarify their responsibilities and the boundaries within which they must operate:

- What outcomes do I own?
- With whom must I work to achieve those outcomes and what are our respective roles?
- What decisions can I make, must I make, and must I cede?
- What rules of engagement govern those with whom I work and me?
- How is my success measured?

Clear, firm boundaries are not limiting; quite the opposite. Firm boundaries set us free. Free to take responsibility, make decisions, and act with confidence.

Of course, it is also critical for all of the ships of an organization to be heading in the same direction. Thus, employees must also know:

- Where are we headed?
- What are our top priorities?
- What does success look like?
- What is my role in helping us get there?

A clear destination, coupled with clear roles and responsibilities, launches strong ships and prevents the flotilla from breaking up or getting lost. Can your employees answer the questions above? Do their answers jive with yours and those of other employees? Are you all headed in the same direction?

Leaders Don't Wait and 7 Other Traits

We all have so much to do that setting our sights on anything above surviving the daily rush can seem unthinkable. Thus, organizations without strong leaders surrender to the daily struggles and believe that tomorrow or next quarter or next year will be a better time to start making changes. Unfortunately, tomorrow is always tomorrow. That's why leaders insist on starting today. Leaders don't wait.

1. Leaders Create Time By Creating a Shared Vision

If you create a shared vision of a better future state, you will generate energy, commitment, and time people didn't know they had. If people are excited about a better future, their excitement propels them forward. They find a way. They become more productive. They see habits that should be crushed and tasks that should be dropped. They cooperate and ask for help. They propose new methods and discover shortcuts. With determination and focus, people can achieve amazing things. Leaders create that shared vision that inspires people to find a way.

2. Leaders Focus

If you have too many priorities, you have no priorities. You must keep the list short so people can focus. Those tough decisions – what not to do, what to outsource, what to postpone, and what to do less well – are critical. Leaders create that focus for themselves and others.

3. Leaders Raise the Bar

Think you are pretty good? Settling for pretty good? If you grew at 20% last year, maybe you didn't set your goal high enough. Leaders expect success to be a stepping-stone to greater success, not a pot in which to grow complacency and arrogance. They celebrate success and then raise the bar.

4. Leaders Have the Courage to Take Risks

Certainty doesn't exist, never has, and never will. There is always more to learn. There is always one more experiment to run. One more person to ask. All of which leave you in pretty much the same place you started – uncertain. You have to take prudent risks. Leaders have the courage to act.

5. Leaders Forgive

Failures are inevitable. Actually, make that essential. If you try something new, you risk failing. But you must forgive yourself and others when this occurs because not trying is the kiss of death. The status quo is the road to mediocrity, shrinking margins, and lost customers. Leaders forgive and keep trying.

6. Leaders Learn

With every success, big or small, you need to celebrate and learn. Figure out how you can replicate, amplify, or accelerate that success. With every mistake or missed opportunity, you need to learn. Figure out exactly what went wrong so you can avoid suffering the same fate once again. Leaders learn constantly from both successes and failures and insist others do likewise.

7. Leaders Know Comfort Zones Are Meant to be Broken

People learn little to nothing when they relax within their comfort zones. Step outside those zones and growth comes fast: new perspectives, increased self-confidence, stronger skills, greater understanding, new ideas, clearer vision, greater determination, increased tolerance – to name a few. Take care of your own growth first by taking on new challenges, going new places, meeting new people, and generally putting yourself in new situations. Give your employees new opportunities and encouragement to do the same. If you make growth safe and expected, your employees will thrive and so will your business. Leaders don't let comfort zones hinder growth.

8. Leaders Don't Wait

Don't wait until the time is right. It never is. If you insist on getting all your ducks in a row, you'll never make a move; ducks just aren't that well behaved. Besides, some of them should be flushed and scattered. If you are serious about progress, whatever direction you are headed, start today. Make a commitment. Ask for help and cooperation. Identify the first step. Start the ball rolling today. Leaders simply don't wait.

Clear Distinctions: Managing People vs. Managing Change

Don't manage change! Manage people!

From my experience, both as a consultant and as an employee, the minute leaders decide change management is necessary is the minute things get weird. Those determined to manage change often see change as a major hurdle, grounds for rebellion, and a most unpleasant and fearsome task. To fortify themselves against the imagined upheaval and resistance, they turn their attention to the 'change process,' which often includes actions such as:

- Developing a communications plan to control what everyone hears and when they hear it.
- Scripting talking points for managers so they all deliver the same scrubbed messages.
- Creating opportunities for the leaders to be highly visible voicing the same messages.
- Planning a big launch to set the stage for change and generate enthusiasm.

With these acts, they create more resistance than they prevent. Furthermore, they invest a ton of energy into activities that add little value to the process of identifying and implementing the actual changes needed.

The most important requirement of change, no matter the scope, is to be sure employees understand what must change and why. That starts at the top, of course. The senior team absolutely must understand what needs to change and why. Scripted messages can't hold a candle to real understanding that naturally creates support and a sincere willingness to be part of the process.

The next level also must understand what and why, though their 'what' will be slightly different because what must change depends on their specific responsibilities and the people they work with most closely. This process must be repeated until everyone understands what needs to change in their neck of the woods and why.

Those who focus on managing people well, rather than managing change, are far more likely to bring the excitement of new opportunities to their teams and involve them in determining what the changes really mean and how to best tackle the challenges involved. This honest, collaborative approach doesn't pretend to have all the answers, it doesn't control information, and it doesn't waste energy on hype. It sees employees as vital players who must be involved in determining how the changes can be made, not as potential resistors or threats to progress.

It also doesn't treat change as a rare bird that visits infrequently. Good managers are always overseeing change, seeking change, and initiating change, and they know how to keep people apprised of what is changing and why.

The more skilled you are at managing people, the more easily you can make changes, whether strategic or operational, whether large or small. And since change is both inevitable and constant, this is a skill worth honing.

Don't let change management become the focus of your efforts. Focus instead on ensuring everyone knows what must change and why.

Clear Distinctions: Fair vs. Equal

My clients strive to be fair to their employees. Where they struggle is in the distinction between fair and equal. The goal is to treat people fairly, not equally.

Equal means the same. Identical. But employees are like snowflakes; no two are quite alike. They don't all need the same level or type of support to succeed. Nor do they want or deserve the same opportunities. They come from different backgrounds and never contribute in exactly the same way. Furthermore, employees don't even like to be rewarded in the same way. Equal treatment does not necessarily make sense.

Fairness, however, is a worthy goal. When people believe they are being treated fairly, they can relax and focus on the priorities and challenges they face. When they feel unfairly treated, their focus shifts completely and they devote more energy to protecting their own interests than tackling important priorities.

Equal may or may not be fair, but fair is always fair!

Want to know how to ensure employees are, and feel, fairly treated?

There are four basic characteristics of a fair environment:

1. Employees know how the game is played.
2. They know where things stand.
3. They see the decision makers as informed and motivated by the best interests of the organization.
4. They know how to influence the process if they question the fairness of actions.

A Fair Process

1. How the game is played

To a large extent, knowing how the game is played involves understanding who makes what decisions, how those decisions are made, and how to participate. Personnel decisions provide excellent examples:

- What employment levels and pay grades exist?
- What responsibilities or other criteria distinguish those levels from one another?
- Who makes those decisions?
- What is the process used for identifying individuals who deserve promotions?
- What do I do if I believe I am deserving?
- How do I know I am not being overlooked and that those criteria are being applied consistently?

This clarity of process applies to other areas as well, not just personnel issues, and is the foundation of creating a culture of fairness.

2. Where things stand

Knowing how the game is played is a critical starting point, but employees also need to know the score. To continue with the personnel example, questions about the score may include:

- What decisions are being made about me?
- What is expected of me?
- How am I doing?
- Who will be providing input for my review?

However, the score may have broader implications than you think and involve everything from company strategy to fairly narrow improvement efforts. In those cases, people need to know what decisions are being made so they aren't blind-sided by changes affecting their work. Being blind-sided erodes trust. No one likes sudden surprises that upset expectations and routines.

3. Informed and fair-minded decision makers

Uninformed decision makers come in three flavors. Some truly are uninformed. Others just appear uninformed. The third group doesn't care to be informed; they are not motivated to do what's best for the organization, and they don't care much about interests of other employees. Unfortunately, all three types undermine the trust and confidence of employees. They are seen as unfair or stupid or both. Employees want to know that the decision makers:

- Understand the impact of pending decisions.
- Know who will be affected.
- Are getting input from employees representative of those who will be affected.
- Will apply rules and decision criteria with consistency and good judgment.
- Care to make decisions that are in the best interests of the organization as a whole, not a particular department, level, or initiative.

4. How to influence the process so bad decisions and poor process aren't repeated

We can tolerate bad decisions if we trust the process. We are even more forgiving if we believe we can prevent a recurrence. If employees think any of the above characteristics of fair process fail, they need to know with whom they should speak.

Make a habit of satisfying these four needs and your employees will see decisions and the process as fair.

Three Traits of Top-Notch Leaders

Top-notch leaders share three essential traits. Two of these traits are well-understood, common targets of conscious improvement, and the topic of numerous articles published daily. The third is another matter entirely. It is not well understood and is rarely discussed in helpful, instructive ways. That's too bad because it offers the single greatest opportunity to improve results and productivity.

1. Respect

How you treat people matters. It matters a lot. Top-notch leaders know this. And while the Internet is filled with advice about how to treat employees, it all boils down to one word: Respect.

If you respect your employees, you:

- Treat them as partners who have something important to contribute. Because they do. If they don't have something to contribute, you recognize the mismatch between position and employee. You don't judge them. You help them find a better match. Because you know you are doing no one a favor by keeping them in a position where they can't succeed.
- Listen. Carefully. Because their expertise, perspectives, and positions differ from yours. You can learn from them.
- Don't make assumptions about their invisible characteristics such as ambition, talent, and attitude. Instead, you focus on their observable behavior and its impact. And you help them develop the awareness, skills, and habits that will amplify their ability to be more effective.
- Respond with compassion, honesty, and pragmatic assistance. Not power or condescension or dread.

That's it in a nutshell for respect. Top-notch leaders are respectful and encourage it in others.

2. Self-awareness

A second trait of top-notch leaders is self-awareness. Great leaders know that self-awareness is essential to their effectiveness. They weren't born on a special planet. They haven't always been models of self-discipline and productivity. They haven't always been satisfied or proud of how they've handled every situation. They've made their share of mistakes. They've lost their tempers and said stupid things.

But one thing they have in common is constant attention to their own behavior and its impact. Top-notch leaders study themselves and the people around them to see themselves through the eyes of others. They want to learn why they do what they do, what works and what doesn't, how to control their least productive instincts, and how to handle every situation better.

How you manage yourself matters just as much as how you manage others. Top-notch leaders know this well and many are also quite good at developing self-awareness in others.

And, once again, there is plenty of literature on this subject for those eager to improve.

3. Clarity

The third trait of top-notch leaders is clarity. Top-notch leaders have excellent clarity. They are clear about their purpose, priorities and next steps. They collect information, weigh risks, and make decisions quickly. They understand their people's capabilities and assign and align responsibilities remarkably well.

But here is the rub. While great leaders have excellent clarity, they can't fathom why others don't. And it frustrates them greatly.

Furthermore, when it comes to creating clarity, they are unconsciously competent. In other words, they do it, but don't really know how they do it. Thus, they can't teach it effectively. And they can't understand why their otherwise highly capable employees just don't 'get it.'

One reason is because creating clarity involves cognitive processes. Cognitive processes move ideas and decisions. Most people don't even think in terms of processes when they think about ideas and decisions. To most people, processes only describe the movement of physical objects.

For example, if you ask people to demonstrate and explain the process of tying a shoe or baking brownies, most could easily walk you through a fairly simple list of concrete steps. Many would even teach you some special vocabulary to clarify the process. Things like 'bunny ears' and 'greasing the pan.' Not only would the explanations be pretty clear and accurate, they would be quite consistent from person to person. And if two people collaborated on a response, they would have no trouble clarifying the process together because of their underlying familiarity with the steps and a shared vocabulary.

Now ask the same people to demonstrate and explain the process of making a decision. I guarantee you won't get crisp explanations or consistency despite the fact that they all make decisions far, far more often than they tie shoes or bake brownies!

While clarity is an essential trait of top-notch leaders, this is the trait where even excellent leaders most need to improve. Imagine how much more effective they, and their staffs, would be if they could move ideas and decisions as easily as a they tie their shoes. Imagine having a shared vocabulary and clarity of process for a multitude of daily activities that aren't even thought of as processes. Go back and read the *Clarity of Process* section for some ideas on how to improve process vocabulary and clarity.

The greatest opportunity to improve corporate productivity resides in clarity. Great leaders have it. If only they knew how to share it!

Clarity Quiz – What is the Best Way to Motivate Employees?

What is the best way to motivate your employees?

1. Reward them financially.
2. Recognize them in public.
3. Recognize them in private.
4. Remove obstacles to success.
5. Give them jobs they love.
6. Explain the value of success.

Make your selection and then read on.

If you chose #4, #5, #6, or all three of those, congratulations! Those are great answers.

When we are doing something we love, we don't need recognition or rewards. Both might be nice, but when we really love the activity, we are naturally energized and eager to continue. If, in addition, we experience discernible progress and success, we are likely to keep on plugging. If, on top of that, we believe the goal is important, people better get out of our way!

Even when we don't love the activity, progress, success, and that feeling of making a valuable contribution can generate that fire that keeps us going.

Thus, leaders should strive for employees who are intrinsically motivated to do a great job and succeed by:

- Matching employees to jobs that are compelling to them,
- Removing obstacles to success, and,
- Helping employees understand the importance of their work.

Praise has its place in helping employees see and feel their value and the value of their work, but all the praise in the world has little impact if employees dislike what they are doing, believe their work is of little value, and see minimal progress or chance of success. Furthermore, empty praise that doesn't ring true can cause more harm than good.

Public recognition also has its place in giving people a sense of belonging and value, but keep in mind that not everyone appreciates public recognition. And while both public and private recognition can be important, recognition for the wrong reasons is of fleeting value at best.

If you concentrate on removing obstacles and helping people succeed, the opportunities to celebrate will be more frequent, more genuine, and of much greater significance to all involved.

Plenty of studies have shown that money is the least motivating of all (unless the employee is struggling to make ends meet). Pay increases generally produce a temporary bump in productivity, if anything. Installing better lighting can have the same effect.

So why do organizations spend so much time and energy playing around with rewards and recognition? Beats me!

In Conclusion – Respectful Leaders Win

Respect tops my list of leadership advice. When you respect people, you are more likely to treat them fairly, like partners, and with compassion. You are more likely to approach them with a win-win attitude and sincere efforts to make mutually satisfactory decisions. And you are more likely to listen – really listen – so you can understand their perspectives, ideas, and concerns. While decisions won't always please everyone, honest respect generates smart decisions, acceptance, and commitment.

Clarity for Accountability

"Holding others accountable successfully requires seeing yourself as a partner in pursuit of mutual success."
Ann Latham

You won't be effective managing others, gaining their commitment, or holding them accountable unless you see yourself as an accountability partner involved in a totally positive process and seeking mutual success.

Top Accountability Mistake

Accountability is a top priority for good reason. But in my experience, efforts to hold people accountable often go off track and do more damage than good.

Accountability Mistake #1 (and only 1): Forgetting the point

When speaking of accountability, one mistake eclipses all others. Too often supervisors at all levels seem to forget that the point of accountabilities is success, not control, not punishment, not blame, not personnel file reports, and certainly not failure. Presumably, you and your employees are on the same team!

If you are holding someone accountable, you are an accountability partner and you should be partnering for success!

The Accountability Process

Accountability Process Step #1: First things first

Since the purpose of accountabilities is to increase the odds of success, the first step is to ensure employees understand:

- What is expected of them.
- That it is their responsibility to seek the structure, support, and feedback they need to be successful.

Thus, accountability partners, whether bosses, co-workers, or friends, must:

- Establish and test for understanding of expectations.
- Offer structure, support, ideas, and advice.

Accountability Process Step #2: Provide structure and support

Behavior is driven by knowledge, attitude, and skill. Every behavior , or action, has an impact and the impact can be small or large, negative or positive. The person whose behavior caused the impact may or may not see or feel repercussions from the impact. Either way, there are lessons learned that affect the person's knowledge, attitude, and skill, which in turn drives future behavior. I call this the *Performance Circle*.

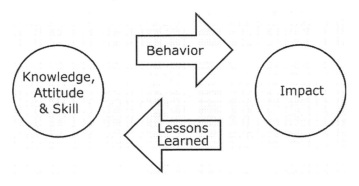

Accountability partners are instrumental in turning a *Performance Circle* into a *Success Circle*. The goal is to increase employee self-awareness by helping employees recognize their own obstacles and helping them find ways to overcome those obstacles. By interjecting Support and Structure as seen in the next diagram, accountability partners help employees modify their behavior so that it results in increasingly positive impact.

Accountability partners do not coax, nag, or do the employee's work for them.

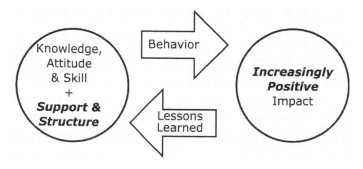

Accountability Process Step #3: Provide feedback

None of us can learn without feedback. Accountability partners help ensure employees seek and get the feedback they need to understand what they are doing, how well it is working, and what they might do to improve. Accountability partners may or may not actually provide the feedback themselves, but they ask questions and offer suggestions to ensure employees get positive and constructive feedback. By interjecting feedback, accountability partners ensure the lessons learned from previous behavior are effective and increase skill, confidence, energy, and trust. The addition of support and structure plus feedback transforms the *Performance Circle* into a *Success Circle* that provides constantly improving results.

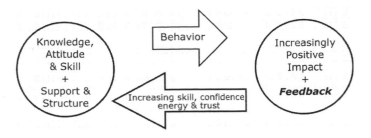

Accountability Process Step #4: Resolve irreconcilable differences

If an employee can't succeed in the current position, an accountability partner helps employees recognize the mismatch. There should be neither surprises nor shame involved. Mismatches between an individual and the needs of the position occur, and when they do, it is as much the fault of the manager as the employee. Help employees succeed by helping them make a match that is likely to be successful.

Who is Responsible for Profitability?

Organization charts and goals can be extremely hazardous to profit margins. You may wonder how this can possibly be, especially when there is usually a great deal of focus on cost cuts. The reason? Not all revenue dollars are created equal and not all cost cuts increase profits. With everyone responsible for something other than profits, profits suffer:

- The sales force is responsible for booking orders; big orders and lots of orders are what counts. They may not have any idea which customers and products are most profitable.
- The production people are responsible for shipping quality products on time. The more products that go out the door on time, the bigger their bonuses and raises. It doesn't matter how many of those products have low or no margin.

181

- The purchasing and inventory folk want the best deal on every purchase while keeping inventory low. Their raises depend on it. Important, high revenue projects and customers might influence their decisions, but beyond that, all lead times and savings are created equal. How much time do they devote to low margin products, making the margins even worse? Are their deals hurting the lead times of high margin products that need to be flying out the door?

- The product development crew ought to be focused on cost effective products, but are they? Are engineers from different groups working together to minimize development, installation, and maintenance costs? Or are they creating super cool products to wow the customer, beat the competition, and attract big bucks?

So now we come down to the CEO and the rest of the executive team. Surely they are responsible for profitability!

The executives better know exactly what is and isn't profitable and why, so that low margin products and customers do not persist without a really good reason. And they better make the tough decisions needed to keep profits strong.

Nonetheless, how much control do the executives have if everyone else can achieve their goals and earn a bonus or raise regardless of margins? In most companies, all the groups mentioned can personally thrive while profits go down the tubes.

Everyone plays a role in company profits. Everyone needs to be responsible for a piece of it. And at the top, the data must be there, the analysis must happen, the tough decisions must be made, and the goals and responsibilities needed to support growing margins must be driven into every corner of the organization.

You Don't Want Compliance

At a client's staff meeting recently, we had an interesting discussion about accountability. When someone stated that accountability and adherence to policy and rules were critical, the result was a combination of vehement agreement and visible discomfort, often on the same face. Why? Because this single sentence combining 'accountability' and 'adherence to policy and rules' in the same sentence muddled an important distinction: accountability and compliance.

- Accountability demands ownership. Compliance demands obedience.
- Accountability puts the focus on outcomes. Compliance puts the focus on rules, policies, control – how things are done – often at the expense of what is achieved.
- Accountability creates a level of autonomy as to how results are achieved, which increases a sense of ownership, determination, and creativity. Compliance strips any autonomy, transfers responsibility to the controlling forces, and encourages a 9 to 5 mentality.
- Accountability allows people to excel, fail, learn, and celebrate success. Compliance causes people to withdraw, take minimal risk, and generally avoid punishment.
- Accountability invests time, energy, and talent in the challenges of producing great results. Compliance invests time, energy, and talent in the challenges of watching each other and perfecting the rules.

I am not saying policies and rules are meant to be broken. I am suggesting you examine your culture and your policies and rules:

- Are you trying to control people or provide them with the freedom they need to excel?
- Are you focused internally or externally?
- Are your employees worried about protecting themselves or are they trusting and open?

183

- Are working conditions (e.g., parking slots, office size and position, flexibility) a sign of status, authority, and privilege, or are they meant to maximize the effectiveness of each employee?

A compliance culture made sense during the Industrial Revolution. It makes no sense today. You do not want a culture of compliance. You want a culture of accountability. You want to maximize each employee's sense of responsibility, determination, and ability to make smart decisions. You want to make growth and success your focus, not adherence to rules. If you need a stronger culture of accountability, get started today.

Uncommon Clarity® in Tracking Progress

Whether you are managing a corporate giant or a small business, you need to track progress. For some, that means tracking key results, for others, it means tracking endless detail. Here are seven tips for maximizing results and minimizing effort.

1. **Don't just track results, track assumptions.** Success for the wrong reasons is not success. If your sales numbers are increasing exactly as desired, but you are growing through increased sales to existing customers and not new market penetration as planned, you have a problem. Your luck is masking failed insights, decisions, efforts, and investments. Be clear about underlying assumptions and ask, "Are our assumptions still valid?"

2. **Define milestones that reflect major decisions and vital learning**, not just the completion of tasks, especially fairly predictable tasks. Keep asking, "What don't we know? What obstacles must we yet overcome?"

3. **Don't let a growing list of checked off milestones give you false confidence.** It's the milestones that aren't checked off that can sink your ship. The easiest are easily completed first. Keep asking, "What could go wrong?"

4. **Every pursuit encompasses uncertainty and risk.** As you learn, you must adapt. Keep asking, "What have we learned and what is its significance?"

5. **Detailed plans give the illusion of control.** Don't be fooled, especially where the detail is no more than a stab in the dark. Keep asking, "How do we know we are on track?"

6. **Even mundane, predictable efforts can go astray because nothing happens the same way twice.** Keep asking, "What has changed? What is different this time? What are we taking for granted?"

7. **Review progress as often as you can afford to be behind.** If you can afford to lose a month, check in once a month. If you can't afford to lose a day, check in daily. "Have we made a day of progress? If not, why not? What must we do differently?"

Uncommon Clarity® in Delegating

Delegating focuses the right people on the right things. It also helps employees to grow. But it is hard. Why? Three reasons: it involves trust or the lack of it, it creates fear of poor outcomes, and it requires clarity. As a result, we typically resort to one of three approaches:

1. "It's easier to do it myself," which neither frees us to do more suitable tasks, nor gives employees the opportunity to grow.
2. "I must learn to delegate so here goes," and then we throw the task over the wall with gritted teeth, crossed fingers, and little faith.
3. We delegate and micromanage, driving everyone nuts.

All of these approaches are unproductive, ridiculous, and unnecessary. To delegate more easily and effectively:

1. Get clear about your desired results and any important limitations or requirements. It will always be easier to do it yourself if you don't know what you are asking! If you are having trouble, it may be because you are confusing the ends with the means. (See #2.) What outcome do you want?

2. Separate expected results from expected methods. The former must be clear; the latter may be irrelevant. And remember, just because you don't know how to do something doesn't mean you have to figure it out before turning it over to someone else. If you can define the 'what,' can the other person discover the 'how'?

3. Focus on matching capabilities to task rather than 'measuring' the individual to decide if he is 'good enough.' If you think about brain power and integrity, it gets uncomfortable. If you try to match knowledge, experience, and skill with a specific task or responsibility, it becomes a rational discussion.

4. Consider the individual decisions and steps within the decisions involved in the task. For help on the decision making process, go back and read the paper *SOAR Through Decisions*™. Does the employee need help establishing the decision criteria – the objectives, priorities, and limitations? Does the employee know which are your most important customers, products, or selling points? This knowledge seems basic to managers but is rarely well-communicated to employees. During my software days, engineers were always ready to design lots of cool features that the customer didn't care about. If you take the time to clarify the objectives/decision criteria, you can delegate next steps more successfully.

5. If the task requires significant judgment, delegate only to someone who is fully aware of the decision criteria, the possible alternatives, and the inherent risks of each. For example, don't turn a large IT task over to someone who measures success strictly by technical accomplishments. The software might work in the end, but the organization may be littered with bodies and vacant seats.

6. Talk to the employee about the process he will follow and where in that process it makes sense to get input or feedback from you or others. Creating greater clarity of process will facilitate this; you may want to go back and read that section.

7. Adopt a collaborative attitude so the employee sees getting help as a smart decision not as a sign of failure.

8. Acknowledge, discuss, and manage risks openly. No one grows without risking failure. Create an environment that is prudent but forgiving.

Growing Pains – Three Hazards to Avoid

Growth can wreak havoc on employees and company performance. As companies grow, employees are stretched, morphed, overwhelmed, and trapped. Meanwhile, fundamental company needs are often ignored. But it doesn't have to be this way.

1. Growing into Unhappiness

Growing into unhappiness is totally common. What happens is a long-term, trusted employee grows up with the company, takes on new responsibilities as needed, and does reasonably well in many different roles. Unfortunately, after several iterations, the assigned responsibilities are often far removed from the passion and interests of the individual. This long-term employee could be a founder who winds up as CEO but would really prefer to be immersed in the technology and innovation that made the company succeed in the first place. Or it could be a salesman who now finds himself behind a desk managing others when he would rather be out talking to customers. There are countless scenarios that can end in unhappiness regardless of individual characteristics.

2. Growing into Failure

Not only might these employees grow into positions that make them miserable, they may also find themselves failing. The most important differences among jobs have nothing to do with the things that capture attention: title, salary, status, and office location. The most important differences involve how you spend your time all day every day, the types of decisions you have to make, and your relationships with customers, suppliers and other employees. That CEO who would rather be immersed in technology may not only dread talking to the media and making huge decisions, he may be really bad at it. The salesman turned manager may be far too assertive and impatient to coach others effectively.

Whether disinterested or ill equipped, both find their personal priorities colliding with company priorities. The unhappy and/or uncomfortable CEO may consciously or unconsciously avoid critical activities. While old friendships and management-by-walking-around make good excuses for mingling with the engineers, the real motivation could lie elsewhere. And that amazing, automated tracking spreadsheet didn't just appear. The CEO spent four hours creating it; four hours that would have been better spent talking to critical customers or thinking strategically. The new sales manager is also driven by misguided priorities: contacting customers instead of supporting salesmen and learning about new products instead of learning about direct reports.

Fit is incredibly important. Employees in positions compatible with their interests, natural inclinations, and capabilities are far happier, more productive, and more successful than others.

The most common scenarios that lead to these growing pains all have one thing in common – too little attention to, and understanding of, personal inclinations, motivation, and productivity:

- Company growth – "Someone's got to do it" coupled with, "We can't afford to hire someone new right now."

- Ego, greed, and other personal confusion – "Wow! That's an offer I can't resist!"
- Career climbing drive – "I'm a failure unless I become a CEO!"
- Misguided rewards – "She is fabulous! Let's promote her!"

It is so much easier and seemingly safer to juggle existing employees than to figure out what you really need, determine the strengths of existing employees, and find the right people to fill the gaps. Nonetheless, that's what my most successful clients do.

3. 'Growing Into...' is Only Part of the Problem

We've seen that 'growing into unhappiness' and 'growing into failure' are two hazards to avoid, but as employees move into new roles, they aren't the only ones who can be negatively affected. If you are leaving behind responsibilities you love, it can be hard to let go. But you must. Micromanagement and constant intervention undermine the growth of those taking on your old responsibilities. They need you to get out of their way.

Employees in new positions also need support. Small companies, in particular, are notorious for promoting people into more powerful positions without teaching them how to manage others. You'd be amazed at how often my clients list their main responsibilities and 'forget' to put management on the list. If you have direct reports, management better be on your list!

189

What Should I Be Doing?

As companies grow and individual roles morph to fulfill immediate needs, things can get pretty crazy. Not only do individuals end up in the wrong places, fundamental responsibilities necessary in any organization may be completely neglected.

Level	Fundamental Responsibilities
Executives	Create the future. Coach the managers.
Managers	Ensure all groups, products, and processes are productive, profitable, and working effectively together. Coach the supervisors.
Supervisors	Run the day-to-day business. Coach the workers.
Workers	Deliver as promised.

This stratification isn't rigid. It does not mean supervisors aren't helping to streamline processes or workers can't help identify product opportunities. It also doesn't mean that there won't be some overlap between levels, especially in smaller companies.

But it does mean that someone needs to be looking out for the future, someone needs to ensure profitable execution, and someone also needs to meet customer expectations.

Furthermore, everyone with management responsibility must manage; 'Boss' is not just a title.

Which of these fundamental responsibilities is most neglected in your company? Are the executives caught up in daily affairs? If so, who is ensuring a strong future? Have you migrated into a position that drains or strains your effectiveness? Who would secretly love to return to former responsibilities?

To avoid the hazards of growth, ensure enthusiastic, capable, and realistic ownership of the four fundamental responsibilities. And to minimize mismatches between people and positions, stress fit, effectiveness, and happiness over titles, promotions, and other career climbing incentives.

Create Clarity, Not Rules!

When managers don't know what to do, they often make a wasteful and disrespectful mistake: they try to control people with rules when it is clarity that is needed. Here are some examples:

Rule: You must work a 40-hour week, arrive no later than 8:30am, and take an hour for lunch.

Clarity: You must make discernible progress on fronts A, B and C and alert me to obstacles you can't remove by yourself so I can help and the organization can continue to afford to pay you. If any of these requires you to be on site at 8:30 in the morning, then of course you have to be here. And when you finish A, B, and C, it's time to talk about what comes next.

Rule: Every meeting must have an agenda.

Clarity: Don't start a meeting unless you know what must be different when it ends. A list of topics on a nicely formatted piece of paper does not mean you will walk out of the room with significant outcomes. I want results, not agendas.

Rule: I expect a progress report in my inbox by 9:00am every Monday morning.

Clarity: I need to be sure we are on track to meet the expectations of our customers and partners, anticipating and preventing problems, and dealing with obstacles as quickly as possible. How do you know we will meet those expectations? What must we learn or do to be more certain? What can I do to help? I want results, not reports or excuses. And I certainly don't want you wasting time trying to make it look like you are succeeding when you aren't or waiting until Monday morning to ask for help.

Rule: Our dress code requires...

Clarity: We operate in a conservative industry and often have customers in the building. Thus, we need you to look professional by their standards, which means you need to be better dressed than 75% of them.

Rule: Doors will be locked if you arrive late to a meeting.

Clarity: We wouldn't have invited you if we didn't need you and making people wait is rude, disrespectful, and demonstrates a lack of planning and organization on your part.

Get the idea? Rules really are insulting to employees. You can't tell talented employees that you want them to step up and take responsibility, and then hit them with a rule or a wasteful practice that adds no value. Furthermore, it is so much faster to create clarity. I have had clients who wasted unbelievable amounts of time writing long employee manuals and trying to make dress codes specific enough to be effective. Create clarity, not rules.

What No One Ever Told You About Delegation

When I opened the refrigerator this morning, the space normally occupied by 100% natural orange juice was taken by an alternative. The unnaturally long list of unrecognizable ingredients and pledges of less sugar and calories raised my hackles almost as fast as my hesitation raised my husband's defenses. He thought we could try it. I thought he had flipped.

In some marriages, this could be the burnt toast that breaks the camel's back. Why? Because we shop the perimeter of the grocery store. Our cart contains little other than fresh fruit, vegetables, chicken, and seafood. Since we don't squeeze our own juice or keep a cow, we venture into 'processed' aisles for things like juice and milk. However, the criteria that drive our selections remain constant. The brand of juice and milk matters little; the length and contents of the ingredients list matters a lot.

Since my husband does most of the shopping, harmony depends on a clear and shared understanding of these decision criteria. His criteria and mine are not exactly the same, which is why he often buys things for himself that he knows I am unlikely to eat. Trouble comes only when he buys meals or staples for me based on criteria like 'it looked interesting' or 'it was less expensive' while violating all the other criteria. 'Interesting' and 'less expensive' are not reasons to abandon my priorities, especially not for something as basic as orange juice that I drink every day.

Now imagine if I delegated the shopping responsibilities to someone else without creating this shared understanding. Vegetables swimming in fatty sauces and fish coated with salty breading would disturb the peace purchase after purchase. I'd turn up my nose, send her back, and seriously question her intelligence and judgment. Meanwhile, our shopper would suffer equal parts anger with my pickiness and frustration with her inability to 'get it.'

Well, guess what. A lot of your employees are angry with 'your pickiness' and frustrated with their inability to 'get it.' And they aren't just angry, they are costing you a bundle. The best are leaving or have already left.

When you see a lack of good judgment or a lack of care, that's rarely the problem. The real problem is that you haven't given your employees a good grasp of your objectives – the criteria that must govern their decisions. They don't have a means of assessing success by your standards. They are like my proposed shopper who doesn't understand that my standards for good food require few ingredients and minimal processing. You can't expect people to bring you an alternative you can support if you don't start with a shared understanding of how to recognize a good alternative when you see one. "Bring me a different rock" gets you nothing but a different rock.

In a recent meeting at a major hospital, the director of strategy explained to me that she needed to improve the presentation skills of the people in her group. She went on to explain how her group does great research, develops terrific plans, but then struggles to persuade the executive team to adopt those plans and take action. She sees better presentation skills as the solution. It's not. The problem is that she brought the executives an alternative without first agreeing on objectives. That's like my shopper bringing me a happy meal or fish sticks. Had she worked first with the executives to establish a shared understanding of the criteria that would be used to assess her group's proposal, they'd be in like Flynn regardless of the quality of their presentation skills. But wait a minute! What are these executives thinking when they create a strategy group and then neglect to sit down with them to establish shared objectives? Why hire expensive talent and let them hunt blind? "Nope. Wrong rock. Bring us a different rock."

In another case, a client of mine explained how an executive had asked him to look into a marketing opportunity that involved installing sponsored sun screen dispensers in public parks. He unleashed his group to research vendors, investigate park and rec rules and regulations, estimate start up and maintenance expenses, evaluate current market penetration, and examine similar actions by competitors. Then they assembled a proposal. The time invested in this effort was definitely non-trivial and delayed other important work. What criteria would govern the decision to accept or reject his recommendation? He had no idea. He just developed the best proposal he could. Turns out, no proposal was needed. The request to "look into" the opportunity was impulsive and quickly forgotten. A short discussion about objectives would have saved as much as 100 hours of highly paid effort and kept this team focused on their real priorities. "Nope. Wrong rock. Oops, I guess we didn't even need a rock."

There is one clear distinction at the heart of all of these problems: objectives vs. alternatives.

- Objectives are the criteria that will govern a decision. These include priorities, goals, and constraints. For food, they might include guidelines for additives, processing, or allergies. For strategies, they include things such as time horizons, scope, risk, growth targets, priorities, and assumptions about the economy and future performance. For the sponsorship opportunity, you'd expect business priorities, target markets, product plans, and investment desires.

- Alternatives are the multitude of possibilities that need to be weighed against those objectives. I don't think I have to explain alternatives when it comes to food. For the strategy team, alternatives can run the gamut from huge steps like closing facilities or buying another hospital to more cautious options like modifying the mix of services or changing the nature of the patient-provider relationship by making providers accessible by email. The marketing guy's proposal could nix or support the sponsorship of sun cream dispensers, could propose an alternative sponsorship, or could suggest marketing dollars be used to upgrade the website instead. The range of possibilities is enormous if all you've been given is to "look into it."

The chance of agreeing on an alternative without first agreeing on objectives is about zero. Just ask the strategy team!

If you want to delegate effectively, establish trusting relationships, and develop employee capabilities so they can assume increasing levels of responsibility, you must:

1. Consciously establish objectives separately from alternatives.
2. Recognize that the people most able to establish objectives are not necessarily the same people able to come up with alternatives.
3. Carefully include appropriate people in each of those efforts.
4. Check in on the state of each separately and as needed.
5. Use the objectives as a means of developing employees who are normally caught up only in the alternatives.

Take the personal shopper. You have two choices for managing this situation successfully. Either you provide a detailed shopping list so the shopper doesn't have to make any decisions or you carefully explain your objectives (everything from type of diet to budget) so your buyer will make the same decisions and select the same foods you would. It is unlikely this person would ever influence your objectives. You must decide whether you want him influencing the alternatives.

The strategy team is a different story. The objectives absolutely must be established by the executives and the strategy team working together. If the strategy team is left to establish objectives alone, their proposals will suffer a painful fate: "Nope. Wrong rock. Bring us a different rock." If the executives establish objectives without input from the strategy team, it isn't a strategy team. It's a bunch of order-takers hoping to learn enough about those objectives so they can produce a plan that isn't "the wrong rock."

A high level marketing guy should have a lot to say about the objectives associated with sponsorships, but still needs input from above. Once those objectives are established, it is totally possible that the executives need not be involved again.

A less experienced marketing guy is likely to dwell in the land of alternatives but still needs to understand how the executives are thinking and what would constitute success in their eyes. He also stands to learn a tremendous amount from the discussions that establish objectives and evaluate possible alternatives against those objectives. Consider having him take the first stab at identifying the objectives or give him a first draft and let him flesh it out.

By making a clear distinction between objectives and alternatives, you can involve the right people at the right time and ensure agreement each step of the way. The result will be more successful delegation and the ability to develop the business acumen and skills of your employees.

Clarity Quiz – Who's Responsible for Profits?

Who is responsible for profitability?

1. Sales.
2. Manufacturing/Production.
3. Purchasing and Inventory Management.
4. Product Development.
5. CEO.

Make your selection and see if you are correct.

Did you struggle with this one? It was a trick question as there should be a number 6, that is "All of the above". Keep this in mind, and you will find yourself being sure all employees know what is most important and why. For more information go back and re-read the paper on *Who is Responsible for Profitability?*

In Conclusion – Be An Accountability Partner

Partners win and lose together. It's best to remember that. If you want to hold other people accountable, you need to be their partner. You need to ensure they have the support, structure, and feedback they need to succeed. You don't have to provide it. You certainly don't want to badger them. But you do need to help them find the secrets to their own success and the feedback they need to stay on track and constantly improve their ability to contribute. When they succeed, you succeed. Success begets success for them, for you, and for the company.

Successful employees are also committed employees. Read on to discover how clarity increases commitment.

Clarity for Commitment

"Just because people stop saying no doesn't mean they've said yes.
They may have simply given up."
Ann Latham

Keep in mind that how you make decisions and plans is often more important than what you decide or plan. When people know how the game is played, trust that it is played fairly, believe they can contribute effectively, and see evidence of success, they will trust the process, believe in the goals, strive for success, and feel far more committed to the organization.

Top Commitment Mistakes

With the commitment of others, there is little you cannot accomplish. Without that commitment, you will be lucky to accomplish anything. Creating commitment is essential to productivity, performance, and profits. Let's start with the top mistakes people make when hoping to improve commitment.

Commitment Mistake #1: Confusing consensus with commitment

The pursuit of consensus is time-consuming, unnecessary, often counter-productive, and frequently the path to a watered down lowest common denominator outcome that offends no one.

You can create consensus without creating commitment and you can create commitment without consensus. It is commitment that you want, not consensus.

Commitment rises from how you plan and decide, not what you decide or the number of people you involve. Commitment rises from creating a trusted process that is informed and fair. Without that trust, people want their fingers in every pot so they can try to prevent problems.

Commitment Mistake #2: Pursuing engagement

The problem with employee engagement is that it is based on employee surveys. Employee surveys reflect nothing but opinions and feelings. Organizations collect scads of data on how people feel, but when it comes to doing something about it, they have neither a clue, nor a chance. Changing feelings is a silly activity akin to pushing a rope.

Furthermore, the focus on employee engagement is actually harmful. It encourages managers to seek consensus. It creates a sense of employee entitlement. It disempowers by giving employees 101 survey questions that prove they are helpless victims. And it increases costs by convincing leaders they must pump up benefit programs and buy extras like pizza.

All because they are trying to make employees happy. They are trying to make them feel good. They are trying to make them love their managers. But there is no guarantee that any of these efforts will actually make employees happier. Nor is there any guarantee these efforts will improve business results.

What we need instead is employee commitment. Committed employees are vested in their work, they stick around, they thrill customers, they go the extra mile, they are excited, and when they clear one obstacle, they are fortified and ready to tackle the next. It doesn't matter whether they have fancy offices, high salaries, or whether they like their bosses. And they don't want money wasted on pizza parties either. They are determined and excited to get results.

12 Reasons Why How You Make Decisions Is More Important Than What You Decide

What's the very first decision you make each day? For some it comes while still in bed: "Should I get up or hit the snooze button?" For those who lay their clothes out the night before, have no children, and are locked into an unwavering morning routine, including the content and quantity of breakfast, that first decision of the day can be postponed. Now that I've written that, I'm really curious to know how long someone could actually avoid that first decision. Not that it matters. Avoiding a few dozen decisions in the morning may reduce initial stress, but it's only a drop in the bucket of what's to come.

We make thousands of decisions every day. Many are easy, but others are complex, stressful, or both. Because there are so many decisions and because they are literal forks in the road with dramatic impact on results, costs, time, feelings, and relationships, how you make decisions is extremely important. This is why decision making is a top priority when I work with clients to create a *Culture of Clarity*.

The best way to make decisions involves the four-step process described previously that allows you to *SOAR Through Decisions*™ whether alone or in a group. If your decisions actually follow the four distinct steps of SOAR™ and involve the right people at each of those steps, with transparency, the benefits are numerous and dramatic.

1. You'll make better decisions.

When you conflate the four steps of decision making into one muddled discussion, it stands to reason that you won't make the best decision. Instead, your decisions are more likely to be governed by one of three forces:

- Fatigue – The winner is the most cohesive idea on the table when the energy expires.
- Enthusiasm – The winner is the idea most fervently expressed by the loudest reputable group.
- Authority – The winner is the obvious favorite of the most senior individual.

These forces do not produce sound decisions.

2. You'll save time and make better use of resources.

A lack of process clarity guarantees a slower, more convoluted path to the desired outcome. Or even a disappointing outcome. This is true whether you are doing something like building a boat or making a decision. If you step logically through a proven process, you will waste less time and make use of the right resources at the right time. If you follow a muddled process to build a boat and want expert help for all aspects of the process, you would have to have all the experts present the entire time and they would be stepping all over each other trying to advise you. You would never build a boat that way. You would learn the process, follow it in sequence, and call on the help you needed at each step. So why do you make decisions by hauling all the experts into a room at one time and trying to tackle all the steps simultaneously?

3. All employees will be able to contribute more effectively.

As mentioned once previously, in the healthcare world, there is a proven process called SBAR – Situation, Background, Assessment, Recommendation. Because it is widely known and understood, it creates what I call shared process clarity and gets everyone on the same page quickly, knowing what to expect and how to contribute. Everyone focuses on the same step at the same time. Everyone shares a clear purpose, one step at a time, and overall. As a result, the Situation and each subsequent step can be described with great clarity. Any practitioner with additional information can easily, and confidently, chime in to enhance or clarify any one of the four steps. With this kind of clarity, every employee is able to contribute more effectively. The same benefits accrue when you *SOAR Through Decisions*™.

4. Professional development is enhanced.

This clarity of purpose and process created by SBAR and SOAR™ is also tremendously instructive. Each time one practitioner hears another describe the Situation, Background, Assessment, or Recommendation, he learns and improves his own ability to formulate relevant information. By constantly learning from each other, everyone sharpens their skills. Without the clarity of process and purpose created by SBAR, the conversation would be far more muddled, descriptions of the Situation would be interwoven with Background and Recommendations. Nothing would be as crisp. And the instructional value would be far less.

The exact same principles hold when *SOARing Through Decisions*™. The O in SOAR™ stands for Objectives. These are the goals and constraints – the decision criteria – that must guide the decision. Just think about the developmental value of employees gaining a clear understanding of the criteria guiding the decisions that affect them. It is enormous. That understanding is the road to greater business acumen and the priorities and culture of the company. The same applies to the other steps of this or any other process. The clarity of purpose achieved through well-defined processes provides tremendous learning.

5. People will accomplish more faster.

When you know exactly what you are trying to achieve, you can do it faster. Period. I doubt that requires more explanation. Speed comes from greater clarity of purpose and process. Just picture a group stepping through SBAR outside a patient's room. No time is wasted. Everyone is sharp. You can gain that same crisp, effective efficiency for every decision when you choose to SOAR™.

6. Commitment will be stronger.

Employees are most committed when they believe decisions are made using a logical, informed, and fair process with their interests represented. Go back and read the paper, *Clear Distinctions: Fair vs. Equal* to understand why a fair process is so important. Muddled processes don't provide much evidence of logic, good input, fairness, or representation of interests. Muddled decision processes create skeptics and cynics, not committed employees. On the other hand, if employees believe the people and process were careful and thorough, they will support decisions even when the decisions turn out to be stupid.

7. Employee satisfaction and engagement will improve.

Employee engagement is a hot topic. Employee satisfaction and engagement hinge on how easily and effectively employees can contribute (see #3) and whether the organization operates in such a way that commitment is created (see #6). Since how you make decisions directly affects both of those, it will also affect employee satisfaction and engagement.

8. Employees will be able to let go and focus.

When you don't trust that the people around you are making smart decisions, it is natural to want to be involved in almost everything so you can try to help prevent disaster or at least see it coming and avoid a nasty surprise. This is human nature. At the same time, everyone has too much to do to be effectively involved in everything. By creating clarity of purpose, process, and roles, people learn to trust the system and let go. Once that happens, they can get back to their top priorities and maximize their focus.

9. Delegation will be easier and more effective.

One of the biggest problems with delegation is that delegating almost anything includes delegating decisions. Well, if you treat decisions as one muddled step, your only choices are to do things yourself or throw the task over the wall and hope for the best. However, if all parties have shared process clarity about the steps of making decisions, it is a cinch to delegate a portion of the decision or an entire decision and arrange for check-ins at appropriate steps.

10. Employees will feel a stronger sense of ownership.

I'm working with a Fortune 100 company right now that gets totally stuck on simple decisions. Why? Because they are usually trying to make several decisions at once. This, by the way, is super common and simply means they have skipped Step #1 of SOAR™. S stands for Statement – state the decision you need to make. While they thrash about, it is difficult for anyone to take ownership because no one knows in which direction to go. Exhaustion ensues. Efforts flag. Progress grinds to a halt. All because they skipped Step #1.

Add clarity of purpose and process to this situation and everyone would know what decision they are making, which steps they own, and how to proceed. Clarity is essential to unleashing ownership.

11. People will make fewer mistakes.

Messy decision processes facilitate errors and misunderstandings. The messier your process, the easier it is to reach a misguided decision and the easier it is for someone to walk out of the room with the wrong message about what was concluded and why. You may think you reached consensus, but how could you know unless you reach clear agreement on each of the four steps of SOAR™?

12. Introverts can stop waiting for Godot.

Introverts are notorious for waiting for the right moment to interject their comments. I know because I am one. Since talking isn't an introvert's default behavior, they only talk when they have a purpose and something to say. And if their purpose doesn't match the conversation, they wait for the right time. In a wandering conversation, the right time never comes. It may come close, they may get ready to speak, and then someone takes the conversation in a new direction and they are left waiting for Godot. Godot, of course, never arrives.

Making decisions is essential to progress. Making the absolute best decision may or may not be really important. But how you leave people feeling is almost always important, that's how you gain commitment. Decisions made with clarity produce the best results across the board.

Has The Pendulum Swung Too Far On Seeking Consensus?

Are CEOs, senior executives, business owners, and managers of all stripes seeking consensus too often?

The demise of top down, arrogant, autocratic management is cause for celebration. Many executives and managers have seen the light and now treat their employees with more respect. They have come to realize that employees with differing expertise, experience, and positions within the company can provide valuable and varied input and ideas that facilitate problem solving, improve decisions, lead to more sustainable improvements, and save time. Furthermore, they now believe involving employees in the organization's challenges doesn't just enhance that one particular situation, it also energizes employees, stimulates good ideas, improves employee judgment, and saves time throughout the organization on a daily basis. They also realize there is no shame in not having all the answers themselves and real danger in making important decisions without getting critical input from others. While some old school managers still adhere to the old top-down practices, despite fleeing employees, many executives are now proud of having evolved to being consensus-driven and they now do everything by consensus. And that is where the problem lies. The pendulum has swung too far in many companies.

I encounter executives and managers daily who no longer seem able to make a decision by themselves. I see CEOs take a decision first to one group, then another, and maybe more. The decision drags out for months. The process resembles a fishing expedition, casting here and there, motoring around to different corners of the lake. The result is similar too: another day gone.

In a wandering, consensus-seeking process, decisions are rerouted or derailed entirely for all the wrong reasons and tremendous time is wasted with the involvement of so many people in countless, endless meetings.

There is a huge difference between appreciating the value of achieving consensus and doing everything by consensus. Being consensus-driven is the opposite, and equally extreme, position to being autocratic. Both are wasteful and problematic in any organization. A consensus-driven manager takes pride in gathering people and running meetings, but they likely spend more money evaluating a purchase than the purchase price, more time talking about an option than it would take to just try it, more anxiety hoping to pave the way for a change than it would take to deal with the consequences.

Don't think about being autocratic versus consensus-driven. This is not a personal style issue. There are times when managers should be autocratic, make a decision, and get on with things, and there are times when managers should delegate the entire decision to a group and get out of the picture completely. In between, there are countless variations. The point is to choose one that best fits the circumstances.

In making that choice, there are five factors to consider.

1. Time Available

If the window of opportunity is short, a quick decision is essential. Sometimes it is more important to act than to wait for more information. For example, when a customer complains, the organization that can address the concern on the spot, makes the customer happiest. Or perhaps something pops up that requires an immediate response before the window of opportunity closes. He who deliberates loses. You may wish you could get more input but collecting information takes time.

Ask yourself how the passage of time affects the situation and be sure you decide as quickly as needed.

2. Significance of the Decision

The most important decisions deserve the best resources, the most rigorous process, and adequate time. You don't want to devote more resources than the decision warrants. You don't want expensive resources making trivial decisions. You don't want large groups leaving more important work to make decisions of limited consequence. And, even on an important decision, you don't want to devote resources to debating options A and B if the differences are inconsequential.

Ask yourself how much money it makes sense to devote to the decision and then figure out how to best allocate those resources. A thorough understanding of the steps of the decision process will help you choose and allocate your resources effectively, go back and re-read *SOAR Through Decisions*™ for more information.

3. Knowledge

If you don't possess the knowledge needed to make a decision, you have no choice but to get input from others or live with the consequences. This is where the arrogance of autocrats leads to stupid decisions; they make decisions they know nothing about. This is where the consensus-driven managers waste time and money; they often fish for more opinions without thinking through the best way to identify and collect the most important knowledge and opinions. You will never have all the knowledge you need because there will always be unknowns.

Ask yourself who can best shed light on each step or important aspect of the process and involve those people. Where appropriate, revisit the planning process, *DRAW Your Plans,* and if you are still finding problems, look at eradicating them with the *SPOT Remover.* Just keep in mind the investment you decided was appropriate for the decision.

4. Need for Commitment

Employees usually accept decisions, whether they agree with them or not, if they believe the decision process was fair and informed. To be seen as fair, a decision requires honest, open, and reasonable objectives and deciders who are dedicated to those objectives. A fair process is needed, read *Clear Distinctions: Fair vs. Equal* to understand how to achieve it. To be seen as informed, the deciders must take into consideration important factors such as the impact on those affected by the decision.

This does not mean every affected employee needs to be involved, but it does mean they need to believe their interests were well represented. Furthermore, it does not mean that everyone involved in a decision must be involved in every step of the decision. For example, senior management may decide to cut budgets without input, but when it comes to where specific cuts should be made, others need to be involved.

Ask yourself who will be impacted, how they will be impacted, where their input is most critical, and how you can obtain it. The biggest impact often involves implementation and can be easily obtained with focused discussions.

5. Employee Development

Involving employees in decisions is a great way to develop their skills and understanding of the business. Furthermore, it can pave the way to delegating decisions entirely, which helps move them lower in the organization where they likely belong.

This may sound like an invitation to involve everyone in every decision, but that would be at the expense of everything else they are supposed to be doing. Ask yourself where it makes sense to invest in training because that is what you would be doing.

However, if you want to teach employees to become better decision makers, be sure you model good decision making yourself. This is particularly important with group decisions. There is no point in teaching employees how to flounder through decisions.

If you have gotten in the habit of making all decisions by consensus, it is time to step back and consider the cost each time you hem and haw and assemble a group for a series of meetings.

Are Your Employees Committed to the Wrong Things?

We are most committed to a course of action when we have some 'skin in the game.' We get into the game in a number of ways. One is by investing time and money.

Public announcements of our goals and intentions are another significant way of cementing commitment. It is hard for us to walk away from a plan once we have told others.

I can vouch for this personally. The night before my wedding, I could not sleep a wink. I was wondering whether I was even capable of seeing glaring evidence of folly while the ball was rolling so vigorously toward our wedding day. As guests made travel plans, the word spread more broadly, and gifts began to arrive, the snowball took control. Decades later, I still remember vividly that lesson about the power our prior decisions, public statements, and invested time and money have over our thoughts and options.

This power can be used to garner great organizational commitment. As people devote energy to a goal, make decisions that support that goal, and announce their commitment, they gradually become more and more committed. If we backtrack, we risk seeming unreliable and inconsistent. Worse, we start feeling confused and stupid. Our pride is at stake. We are wired to rationalize our previous decisions. We are masters of painting glorious pictures of the benefits of our choices. And we are incredibly quick to throw more time and money at those goals.

When the direction is good, this power is fabulous, motivating, energizing. With less than optimal decisions, this power helps us make the best of things, which is often the best course.

But when the direction is bad, this power can be overwhelming. It can take tremendous strength to recognize, not admit, just recognize that we have made a bad decision. It can take even more strength to admit it. And even the strongest cower at the prospect of telling others "I was wrong, that was not a good decision. We must abandon this market, product, project, house, wedding, ..., and go in a new direction." But every business and every human makes mistakes. Many are bad. We have to learn to recognize, admit, and reverse those hurting our lives and businesses. What decisions have you made that are better reversed now than later?

Successful Executive Wannabees

I used to play the cello. I guess. Sort of. I say sheepishly. When I listen to beautiful cello music, all I can say is I have a cello, and I wish I could play like that.

So why can't I? I love the cello. I love the way it sounds. I've played it enough to believe I could play well. So why can't I?

- Did I want it really badly, at least compared to other things?
- Did I have any realistic sense of the steps I needed to take to get really good?

212

- Did I have a teacher who not only helped me make progress, but also helped me see and understand my progress, really see and appreciate the importance of my incremental improvement?
- Did I see learning to play as a compelling, enjoyable activity? Or did I see it as a nearly insurmountable, time-consuming chore?

My answers: I guess not. No. No. The latter.

In other words, being an awe-inspiring cellist was just a pretty idea. Most of us have lots of pretty ideas over the course of our lives.

Most businesses do as well. Teams of smart, well-meaning people assemble pretty ideas regularly. They call them visions and strategies. Thick plans follow. But not much else. Not much meaningful change or daily efforts that will allow the organization to make those ideas a reality.

More often than not, the individuals who must do something differently are too much like a cellist wannabe.

They don't want to change that badly and may not understand why it is important. They don't know with sufficient specificity what they need to do differently, including what they need to stop doing. They don't have the support, including the time, to make the necessary changes. Nor are they able to see progress and, thus, gain momentum and enthusiasm from incremental success. And their skills and interests may not align with the new tasks and responsibilities thrown their way.

So they keep doing what they've always done. At least mostly. They think about their jobs in the same old ways.

Who are 'they'? Everyone from shop floor contributors to the inhabitants of the corner office. And business-as-usual prevails.

Meanwhile, the executives are dismayed and irritated. What happened to their pretty idea?

213

Clear Distinctions: Ends vs. Means

Having arrived early for a client meeting, I became privy to a conversation spurred by heavy resistance to changes underway. Those present proposed many ideas to reduce the resistance. Those ideas were of two distinct types, one good and one bad:

1. Changes to the goal.
2. Changes to the methods used to achieve the goal.

If you are struggling with implementation, whether encountering resistance or hitting other obstacles, be sure to distinguish between the ends and the means. If your goal is sound, don't sacrifice it just because you haven't found a suitable method for achieving it. There are always multiple paths to any destination. If your desired end point is important, stay strong and find a new path.

10 Reasons Your Employee Engagement Program Is Hurting Your Company

There is a big problem in corporate America today. According to Gallup's 2016 State of the American Workplace[4], only 33% of employees consider themselves 'engaged' at work. As a result, corporations are embarked on multi-million dollar employee engagement programs in an effort to improve these numbers. Unfortunately, they are barking up the wrong tree. Employee engagement programs aren't the solution to poor engagement.

While there is a high correlation between employee engagement survey results and business performance, there is no proof that the former causes the latter.

---

[4] Gallup developed State of the American Workplace using data collected from more than 195,600 U.S. employees via the Gallup Panel and Gallup Daily tracking in 2015 and 2016, and more than 31 million respondents through Gallup's Q12 Client Database. First launched in 2010, this is the third iteration of the report.

And that's because it doesn't. Engagement, as measured by employee surveys, does not cause success. Engagement is, at best, a symptom of success. Employees who are succeeding and feeling good about their ability to contribute their best to your company are naturally more likely to:

- Be proud to work for your company.
- Be happy to come to work each day.
- Feel valued.

Which leads to high engagement scores. Employees who don't feel like they are getting anywhere and are not happy with their own performance are not going to rate any of these highly.

So if engagement scores go up with improved results, why not just focus on improving real results? And why not focus on making employees more successful so that:

- Projects are finished on time and on budget.
- Employees overcome significant challenges.
- Customer satisfaction and loyalty are strong.
- Productivity is high or improving.
- Top talent sticks around.

Not only is the pursuit of employee engagement barking up the wrong tree, it is worse than that. Here are ten reasons why pursuing employee engagement is destructive:

1. Employee engagement programs are huge, internally focused distractions that create no value for which customers are willing to pay. Imagine adding an "engagement surcharge" to every invoice. How would your customers feel about that? (You'd get them engaged!)
2. Engagement surveys disempower employees by giving them 101 reasons (a.k.a. survey questions) why they are helpless victims in a hopeless environment.

3. Opinions and feelings collected by survey provide no insight into the observable behaviors that must be changed. This leaves management with data but no clue how to make real improvements.

4. The fear of declining survey results encourages managers to manage by consensus, which is a tremendous time-waster in itself.

5. A desire to keep everyone happy leads to innocuous decisions that annoy no one instead of well-informed, smart decisions that might ruffle some feathers.

6. A desire to keep everyone engaged leads to insincere requests for input that will never be used.

7. Employees are not fooled by insincere requests for input so these shams erode trust and further damage that sense of engagement.

8. Managers eager to improve engagement numbers waste money on pep fests and pizza. Or worse, on undeserved promotions and raises.

9. Engagement creates a sense of entitlement among employees who suddenly believe the company owes them a best friend at work, an inspirational manager, a great office, or some other mom-and-apple-pie nicety that will make the workplace perfect.

10. Last, but not least by a long shot, engagement programs invest millions of dollars trying, in a round-about manner, to do what the performance management system is already supposed to be doing: ensuring everyone is in a job where they can succeed, if not excel. In particular, this includes getting rid of bad managers.

So here is what you should do with all that money, time, and energy you are currently devoting, or are about to devote, to an employee engagement program. Concentrate instead on helping your employees be effective and more successful. Let their happiness, eagerness, and energy follow of its own accord. There are three areas for you to focus on:

1. **Ensure clarity of purpose** – Employees must know what they are trying to accomplish, why, how well, and with what priorities and constraints.

2. **Ensure clarity of roles** – Talent and responsibilities must be well-matched so employees feel challenged but with a fair shot at excellence.

3. **Ensure clarity of process** – Employees must understand how the game is played, know where things stand, know how they can best contribute, believe decision makers are informed and fair, and believe they can influence the process if things are going awry.

Focus on creating clarity and you can develop effective, committed employees who:

- Go the extra mile, which leads to projects finished on time and on budget.
- Knock down walls to overcome significant challenges, which in turn increases their pride, confidence, and appetite for another challenge.
- Are determined to help customers succeed, which creates loyal, trusting customers who make more purchases.
- Care about results, productivity, and continuous improvement.
- Stick around, reducing attrition and the expenses and problems associated with trying to replace top talent.

I'd like to think these same employees would refuse to fill out surveys asking about the inspirational qualities of their managers or the existence of best friends at work. These are the people who get things done, scorn the pizza parties, and care little about the size of their offices. You need more of them. What you don't need is employees spending their time thinking and talking about whether management is doing everything right.

Why Your Employee Performance Ratings Are Hurting Your Organization

Most organizations use ratings, whether numerical or labels, as part of their employee performance review process. They should stop.

Why? Because performance ratings don't help employees improve. And, last I checked, that was the purpose of performance reviews.

Give a person a top rating and they have a good chance of becoming complacent or developing a superiority complex. Give a person anything less than a top rating and you will likely make them angry, disappointed, or jealous – all negative emotions. When ratings are present, that's what employees see and remember. We've all been there. Someone hands you a written review, you scan for the numbers. Someone gives you an aural summation, you listen for clues of the numbers. And whether you like the number or not, you aren't really listening to anything else. Even the most valuable, most carefully presented feedback is heard through that roar of anger, fear, or pride – that rush of emotion generated by your year-end grade.

Meanwhile, the rating is often quite meaningless. Some managers will never give anyone 5 out of 5. They just won't. These are the tough graders we met the likes of back in our school days. Other managers, swept up by grade inflation and believing they hire only exceptional employees, never give less than a 4.

And then there are the mixed messages that occur when all the manager's comments slam up against the unforgiving number at the end of the year. I got a call just this past week from a baffled executive. She'd worked extremely hard to do everything she'd been told would help her be an exceptional employee. Her progress was well received, and she was told she had made dramatic improvements. She responded by asking for even more ways she could increase her effectiveness and value. When her review rolled around, she was rewarded with the same rating she'd gotten the year before. Once the anger and confusion subsided, she asked what would have made the difference. The answers were pathetic and included nothing specific or important to the success of the company. Why inflict pointless negative emotions on your employees?

Then there is the employee who got a 3 out of 5 last year. He took the feedback to heart and was doing his best to make improvements. His efforts were rewarded with a 2. Why? Because management knew they couldn't fire a 3, he wasn't ever going to be a good fit for the job, and they had already decided he needed to go. Both the individual and his company had just lost a year.

So let's get clear here:

1. The purpose of any performance review is to be sure employees know how they can develop their talents and energies and use them more effectively to contribute to the organization's success. This applies to every single employee. No rating is necessary.

2. An employee's ability to grow and contribute effectively requires a good match between the employee's talents and energies and the demands of the position. An on-going, honest, respectful conversation with a win-win attitude about where an employee is most willing and able to contribute is essential. If the current position is not a good fit, the employee should not be tortured with fluctuating ratings, left guessing, or slapped with a surprise. Instead, the employee should be actively involved in seeking a new position that would make for greater success, whether inside or outside the organization. This applies to every single employee. No rating is necessary.

Performance management systems with ratings fail both the employee and the organization. If your goal is to improve performance, stop using ratings and embrace these two points.

If your goal is to document failures, avoid lawsuits, and make it easy for managers to shirk the responsibility of helping employees grow and contribute more effectively, I'm sure you will continue to use ratings. Because that's what they are good for.

7 Rules Naturally Clear Leaders Follow When Making Decisions

If you make decisions by consensus, you waste a lot of time. But if you make decisions without sufficient involvement, you won't gain the cooperation and commitment you need for subsequent steps and successful implementation. How do naturally clear leaders thread this needle? They consciously, or intuitively, follow these seven rules:

1. Fair process matters

If people trust and embrace the decision process, they are more likely to trust and embrace the decision. What makes a decision process trustworthy?

- Those who will be affected by the decision know what is being decided.
- They understand how the decision will be made and are confident the right people will be tapped at the right time.
- They know how to participate.
- They believe those making the decision are informed and working in the best interests of the organization.
- They know how to influence the process if it seems to be going awry (e.g., suffering from uninformed decision makers).

2. Process doesn't just happen – someone needs to own it

The natural inclination of most people is to dive into content without first establishing a process. Someone needs to get ahead of the game and explicitly establish and communicate distinct outcomes, steps, and roles that honor the characteristics of a trustworthy decision process.

3. There are only two reasons to include others in any decision

You should only involve people in a decision if you need their smarts or their commitment. While people often fall in both categories, those who only belong to the first group are experts who can help you make a smarter decision. You tap their smarts, not their emotions. The second group consists of people whose behavior is essential for supporting the decision. They absolutely must understand what, why, and how their support can make a difference. You must tap their smarts as well as their emotions.

4. Time is of the essence

The time spent on any decision must be in proportion to the potential impact of the decision. Don't convince yourself that everyone will be affected by every decision. That's a lazy abdication of responsibility. It wastes too much of everyone's time, and all your employees know it.

Furthermore, time is often a luxury you don't have. Windows of opportunity often open and close too fast to allow for inclusive decisions, no matter how consequential. In these cases, you will need to rely on good explanations and your reputation as a champion of transparent and trustworthy process.

5. Different people may be needed for different steps of the process

The reason for establishing clearly defined steps is two-fold and mostly unrecognized, or at least under appreciated:

- Too often, decisions are expected to emerge from a jumbled series of conversations where participants are rarely actually talking about the same thing at the same time. A disciplined process honors the natural, logical, and sequential steps in any decision (SOAR™: Statement, Objectives, Alternatives, Risks). By making these distinctions and proceeding one step at a time, you focus the collective brainpower and never fail to achieve discernible progress.
- Once you think in terms of these four steps, you realize that roles vary depending on the step. For example, an executive may need to approve the objectives with input from implementers, but may then be ready to walk away and trust the rest of the decision to others. The people in the trenches may be best positioned to generate alternatives. Those most affected and accountable for results may be best positioned to select the most promising alternative. And experts may be the best choice for identifying risks. Establishing process steps before diving in is the only way you will successfully involve the right people at the right time.

6. Representation must be explicit

You can't always include everyone who is affected in a decision. The numbers may be too great, the time too short, or the importance unworthy of that investment. The answer is representation. A clear, fair, and transparent process is a prerequisite for allowing one group to represent the interests of others. Both steps and roles must be explicit. People tend to speak only for themselves. If you want someone to work on behalf of others, you must explicitly and repeatedly make that clear to both parties.

7. Authority must be transparent

There are few feelings worse than investing your physical and emotional energy in making a decision only to have your conclusion overruled. All decision participants need to know who is making the final decision. Are they providing input, feedback, making the decision themselves, or helping to drive a group to consensus? Is the ultimate approver an individual, a boss, a small group, or a large group? There is no right answer. There isn't even a preferred answer. But the answer is important. The answer depends on the time available, need for expertise, importance of the decision, number of people affected, and potential repercussions. Regardless of the approach, clarity is critical. Be honest and crystal clear.

As people become accustomed to a transparent, fair process, especially once the entire organization has a *Culture of Clarity*, you'll find more and more people are content to leave decisions to others and trust they will be called upon as needed. Productivity and empowerment increase with clarity. Use these tips to develop fair and transparent decision-making processes.

Clear Distinctions: Stubborn vs. Persistent

I've been called stubborn a time or two, but I swear it is only by people who don't know the difference between stubborn and persistent! I believe we should all avoid being stubborn and strive to be persistent. The world is not an easy place so persistence is essential. Persistence gets us over hurdles, through tough times, past confusion, and farther down the road to success. Stubbornness just gets us into trouble!

If you are persistent:

1. You doggedly pursue results and are willing to consider different ways to get there.
2. You may repeat yourself in an effort to persuade.
3. You ask questions sincerely and listen eagerly for new information.
4. You are eager to learn, are open to new ideas, and will change direction or method upon hearing something new and relevant to the situation at hand.
5. You may drive people crazy with your determination, energy, and relentless pursuit.

If you are stubborn:

1. You doggedly hold to a single position or course of action.
2. You repeat yourself whether anyone is listening or not.
3. You ask few questions and can be quite vocal about how little you care for the opinions of others.
4. You have no intentions of learning, hearing new ideas, or moving away from your firmly stated position or plan.
5. You will drive people crazy with your inability to hear, learn, and change in any way.

To increase commitment, help employees recognize the difference between persistence and stubbornness so that the persistence can be leveraged without the damage caused by stubbornness. To me, the difference is enormous, and I hope it is clear to you! I also hope I don't drive you too crazy with my determination, energy, and relentless pursuit of results!

Clarity Quiz – What Is The Best Way To Create Commitment?

What is the best way to create commitment?

1. Invite everyone to frequent communications meeting.
2. Make sure everyone feels heard.
3. Launch initiatives with great enthusiasm.
4. Collect ideas from lots of employees.
5. Develop an employee engagement program.
6. All of the above.
7. None of the above.

Make your choice and then see if you are correct!

Did you choose number 7? If so, great job! Communications meetings can play a role, but they aren't nearly enough. Making people "feel they've been heard" is called manipulation. Fanfare might work for new employees, but chances are that previous fanfare has made skeptics of those who've been around a while. Collecting lots of ideas can do more damage than good, unless you implement a good number of those ideas. You already know what I think of employee engagement programs from *10 Reasons Your Employee Engagement Program Is Hurting Your Company* earlier in this section!

In Conclusion – Commit To Gaining Commitment

Commitment stems from success and fair treatment. To increase commitment, focus on ensuring that employees:

- Are challenged with suitable work.
- Have the support they need to succeed (see *The Accountability Process*).
- Believe decisions are made by informed individuals with the right kinds of input and in the best interests of the company.
- Know how to behave, make suggestions, protest, or otherwise play the game so they can contribute their best, prevent problems, and drive improvements.
- Aren't blindsided by decisions that affect their work or environment.

Clarity for Feedback

"Tiptoeing around an employee is the sign of an approaching birthday or a person in the wrong job."
Ann Latham

Focus on observable behavior, its impact, and helping others see what you see. Do not make comments or assumptions about personal characteristics that are invisible.

Top Feedback Mistakes

We all need feedback to learn and improve. If you know how to provide effective feedback and can approach giving feedback with a positive, problem solving, helpful attitude, it can be quite easy. But if you are afraid of it, don't really know how to give or think about feedback, and fall into the many common traps, giving feedback is a nightmare for you *and* the person you offend, anger, and demoralize. Take some time to embrace the concepts and techniques in this section and pair it with what you learned from reading *Clarity for Accountability* and your anxiety and procrastination for giving feedback will both decrease.

Feedback Mistake #1: Confusing assumptions with facts

Which of the following are observable?

- Joe has a bad attitude.
- Katie is ambitious.
- Alex is rude to his co-workers.
- Chris takes pride in his work.
- Casey plays favorites.
- Jordan wasted a lot of time today.
- Kai acted pleased with his group.
- I saw Riley take a lot of notes at the meeting.

If you think *any* of these are observable, you are confusing a lot of assumptions with facts!

Rethink these. What might you actually see that would lead to these assumptions? You can't see an attitude! You can't see ambition, rudeness, or pride! All you can see are behaviors that lead you to make assumptions about attitude and ambition. You can't even see wasted time. And unless you read Riley's notes, you can't be sure she took them. She could have been doodling, working on a report, or writing a letter.

Feedback Mistake #2: Confusing praise with feedback

My mother used to sing "Accentuate the Positive" and you'd do well to do the same. The point of feedback is improvement and above average performers can benefit from feedback just as much as under-performers. We all need feedback to learn so don't forget to tell employees what they are doing well and why it is good so they can make a point of doing the good stuff more often and even better.

But don't confuse praise with feedback. "Great job" is not feedback. "Great job" is praise. If you want to help employees do better, you need to be specific. You need to tell them specifically what they did and why you think they did a good job.

Focus On The Observable – The Problem With Confusing Visible And Invisible Characteristics

Consider these phrases. Do they sound familiar?

- George has no ambition.
- Sarah takes pride in her work.
- Bill has a bad attitude.
- Connie cares only about herself.

Statements like these are super common and frequently tossed about and treated as simple facts. And that is a big problem because it demonstrates a complete lack of clarity about the distinction between visible facts and conclusions drawn about completely invisible characteristics.

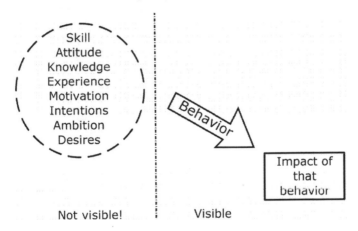

The previous comments address characteristics on the left hand side of this diagram, all of which are completely invisible.

- You cannot see ambition; you can only see behavior that you interpret as ambition or a lack of ambition.
- What you interpret as pride may be perfectionism.
- You may think you 'see' a bad attitude but what you see is behavior that is probably a symptom of other things you can't see such as Bill doesn't like his job, doesn't feel that he can succeed, or is dealing with stressful conditions at home that you know nothing about.
- Connie may seem to care only about herself but the reality could be that she is painfully shy or has been abused in the past.

Any statement about invisible characteristics is a personal opinion, an assumption, a judgment.

However, you can see the way a person behaves. And you can see the impact of that behavior, whether positive or negative, whether it affects you, others, or the entire company. If you focus your attention and comments on that which is visible, the observable behavior and its impact, and leave the speculation about cause out of the picture, you will:

- Avoid destructive comments.
- Prevent putting others on the defensive.
- Help others understand their behavior and its impact.
- Set the stage for involving the other person in improving the situation.

Take another look at the diagram. Think of all the other words that could be added to the circle of invisible characteristics. Words like experience, confidence, and intelligence. There are innumerable possibilities.

Clearly, you know less than you think!

Feedback Process

If you want to help employees do better, you need to provide specific feedback. They need to know specifically what they did and why you think they did a good job.

Feedback Step #1: Seize the day

Don't wait! The point of feedback is to help someone learn how to get better results.

If I ran my canoe into a rock unnecessarily, an immediate explanation of what I did and what I could have done differently is far more effective than trying to accurately resurrect the memory later and talk about how I might have used a different stroke. If I didn't understand the impact of my mistake – the potential danger of hitting that rock – better to explain that to me while I'm standing next to the noisy, rushing water, than back in the comfort of my living room.

Seize the day. Don't let teachable moments get lost in business as usual.

However, before you seize the day, take a look around. Is it safe to interrupt? Do you need to find a private place to avoid causing embarrassment? Is the individual so shaken by the rock and accompanying danger that listening is out of the question now? Use your head. Find a time and place that will maximize the likelihood that the employee will be receptive. Just don't wait any longer than you have to!

Feedback Step #2: Focus on behavior and impact

The key to effective feedback is to focus on specific observable behavior and the impact of that behavior and to do so with specificity. People need to understand specifically what they did and why it matters, whether because the impact was positive or negative. Here is the formula:

231

When you did *(specific behavior)*, I/the company/our group *(the specific impact)*.

This is a fact-based, non-judgmental statement about what occurred. This is the starting point for effective feedback.

"When you interrupted me in the meeting today, I felt as if I must have been saying something stupid or inappropriate."

"When you arrived late today, there was no one to tell our most important customer when they could expect their shipment."

"When you adjusted the spacing of your hands on the bat, you hit it out of the park."

Useless and worse than useless feedback, respectively, look like this: "Great job" and "Don't be so rude." Neither of these tells anyone what specifically needs to be done differently and why.

Note, if the impact of a behavior is not important, or you can't explain why it is important, you need to rethink the situation and your reaction. Quirky behavior is just quirky behavior. A method that differs from yours is just a method that differs from yours, unless you can show that it produces inferior or less reliable results or you've gone to great lengths to develop a reliable process to avoid variations with potentially serious consequences.

Feedback Step #3: Shut up and listen

Once you've provided a factual account of what you saw (the specific observable behavior) and why there is cause for concern (the impact of the behavior), preferably to a receptive employee, it's time to hear the other side of the story. There is so much you don't know!

- Whether the employee knows what is expected ("Really? I'm sorry. I didn't know I was supposed to do that.")

- What the employee thinks he did ("I thought I was following your instructions.")
- Whether the employee realizes he did what he did ("Do I interrupt?" "Am I really slower than everyone else?")
- Whether the employee understands the impact of his behavior ("Wait a minute. Why is that a problem?")
- Why he did what he did ("Joe told me the plan had changed.")
- Whether he has the knowledge and skill needed to do better ("I'm not very good at that part so I figured out a new way that works better for me.")
- What's going on in his life that may preclude doing his best ("I'm sorry. My mother has cancer and I'm having a hard time concentrating.")

Now that you both have a better understanding of what happened and why, you can move on to next steps.

Feedback Process Step #4: Get into problem-solving mode

The goal is to help the employee improve. And that's all you can do. Help. You can't force a change, at least not effectively. All you can do is help the employee figure out what will make him or her do better. Depending on the situation, you may want to ask:

- What might prevent this happening again?
- Would you like me to show you how to do it?
- Would you like to tell me about your approach and I'll see it I can help?
- What might help you learn to do this better?
- What could you do to be sure you don't forget next time?
- Why do you think this is hard for you?
- Would you be comfortable letting the team know you want to break that habit and asking them to provide some kind of gentle reminder when you slip up?

The circumstances are wildly important. Take repeated lateness. If there are temporary extenuating circumstances involving a good employee and a reasonable accommodation, do it. But that's not always the case, and, ultimately, it is the employee's responsibility to figure out how to meet the job responsibilities.

Recipe for Success: Ask Why and Act On The Answer

Over a period of many months, Comcast called me two times to see if I would like to add digital voice. They quoted a great introductory offer and a competitive rate to follow. Calls like this aren't uncommon, but what they did next is surprisingly unusual. When I turned them down, they asked why. I usually have my reasons, yet amazingly, almost no one ever asks.

The first time they called and asked, I told them I didn't want to lose phone service during a power failure. Several months later, we repeated this discussion. Only this time, they had an answer. They would install a battery pack that would allow us to talk for seven hours during a power failure. There would be no additional extra charge. The battery pack would be installed out of the way in the basement. "Can we do that for you on Thursday?"

Perhaps the second caller was simply better informed than the first. However, it is also possible that they are actively collecting answers to their queries of why, looking for solutions to those objections, and calling prospective customers back as soon as the solutions are available.

This shouldn't be so rare!

Increase your sales and improve your offerings with four simple steps:

1. Ask why when your offer is rejected.
2. Track the reasons.
3. Find and make improvements that show a promising ROI.
4. Contact your customers with your improved offer.

And, of course, you don't have to wait for a rejection to get feedback from customers and potential customers alike. Most of us would be happy to share our thoughts and concerns much more often than we are asked as long as the request:

- Doesn't interrupt dinner.
- Doesn't take too long.
- Results in actual improvements.

These caveats may seem obvious, but they aren't judging by my experience. Too often I get calls in the evening and/or am asked to answer long, tedious surveys that never seem to make any difference. The approach Comcast took in this particular case is a good model to follow. No survey, just a decent value proposition and a simple 'Why?'

'Poor Communication' – What Does It Really Mean?

Not sure I've ever encountered an organization that doesn't complain about 'poor communication.' But what does it really mean?

Too often companies respond to the complaint with meetings, memos, newsletters, announcements, presentations, and videos – more communication – without ever touching the real cause of the complaints. When you want to solve a 'poor communication' problem, remember to avoid the three problem-solving mistakes of: leaping to conclusions, confusing problems with wishes, and solving unimportant problems, before delving deeper. The worst thing an organization can do is react inappropriately because they don't know what's really going on. That being said, here are four main reasons why employees complain about a lack of communication:

1. Employees don't know what is important

An unclear strategy and priorities make it impossible for employees to make smart decisions. While poor communication of the strategy and priorities is one possible cause, more often there isn't a clear strategy, the strategy is too complex, and/or there are too many priorities. If there are too many priorities, there are no priorities. If employees don't know what is important, they assume someone is failing to tell them and thus, poor communication is the complaint. This indicates a lack of clarity of purpose.

2. Employees don't know who is supposed to do what when

Ill-defined roles, responsibilities, and processes are another common culprit. Communication may be part of the problem but, more likely, roles, responsibilities, and processes are simply poorly defined. The resulting confusion is annoying at best. People begging for clarification often complain about poor communication.

3. Employees don't do what they are supposed to do

A lack of commitment, discipline, and/or accountability by even a small minority of employees can create the feeling that no one knows who is supposed to do what. You can clarify and communicate roles and responsibilities until you are blue in the face but if employees just do their own thing, confusion ensues, and others will complain about poor communication.

4. Employees don't like surprises that affect their work and lives

The way decisions are made and communicated is often more important than the decision itself if you are affecting employees' sense of security and control. When surprised, even if the surprise isn't bad, a lack of awareness, input, and control often leaves people complaining about poor communication. However, if you let them know a decision is underway and give them reason to believe that their needs are understood and their perspectives are represented, they will accept even bad decisions with fewer ruffled feathers and complaints.

As with any problem, reducing complaints about poor communication requires eliminating the cause of the complaints. Well-intentioned ideas generated without knowledge of the cause have little chance of being effective and almost always waste significant time and money.

To Fire or Not to Fire – Mired in Guilt?

Many of my clients, large and small, share a tendency to keep employees in positions for which they are ill suited far too long. The result is 360 degrees of pain and the solution seems unthinkable. It is time for new thinking.

When an employee is not a good match for the job position, those above, below, and on all sides of the employee in question suffer. The supervisor's expenditure of time, frustration, and anxiety may exceed the total positive contribution made by the mismatched employee. Colleagues of the mismatch may be picking up slack and/or enduring abusive or unpleasant working conditions. Direct reports could be receiving anything from no support to abusive micromanagement. At the very least, they are missing out on a good role model. If you add up the total cost in time, mistakes, missed opportunities, bad precedents, the erosion of energy, the contradiction of company values, and the blow to your own credibility as a leader and manager, the cost of keeping a mismatched employee is huge

Once you realize the full burden of the mismatch, keeping and firing are often seen as the only two choices, and the latter so reeks of surprise and cruelty that it becomes unthinkable. Those beliefs totally cloud our thinking and deserve individual attention.

Let's start with the element of surprise. If you've discussed expectations and provided effective feedback regularly, a mismatched employee should recognize the mismatch as fast, or faster, than you do. And, if you've avoided tiptoeing around the performance and behavior issues, a decision to part ways will certainly not be a surprise, and may be quite mutual.

Second, consider the element of cruelty. In every mismatch, the employee is unhappy, if not totally miserable. Even the wonderfully hard-working, nice employee scrambling to hang on to the job is miserable because the anxiety is a quiet killer. By keeping an employee in the wrong job, you are only postponing the opportunity for a better match and the benefits that only success can bring any individual. While unemployment or economic concerns may make you question the possibility of a better match, don't add one more unsubstantiated belief to the list of factors preventing you from improving the situation for all.

And third, as you've likely heard me say before, there are always more options than first come to mind. Keeping and firing are usually not the only two. Changing the employee's position or responsibilities is often an option. This is particularly true when the mismatch was created by a bad promotion, a far too common occurrence in which the excellent technician is promoted to supervisor or manager, despite having little inclination or aptitude for managing anything other than daily tasks. While egos may seem a formidable barrier to demotion and change, the reality is that egos can heal if given time, space, and a little face-saving positive spin. When I have helped clients make this decision, the collective sigh of relief is audible. Just be sure you don't shuffle a misfit from one mismatched position to another.

Employment is a negotiation between two parties. Employees should seek jobs that fit their strengths and interests, and employers should seek employees who fill their needs. Neither wins when employee strengths and interests are out of alignment with business needs. Work with your employees to discover unhealthy mismatches and explore sensible alternatives. But once the writing is on the wall, gracefully (and legally) help them out the door.

Quit Trying to Be So Nice!

I feel sorry for lots of under-performers. You know the ones. The guys who don't quite measure up but don't understand why because no one has ever told them! One minute they hear what sounds like praise, but it's followed by innuendo and confusing comments.

Most of us have no desire to hurt someone's feelings. So what happens when we have to point out a performance problem?

The natural tendency is to try to reduce the bad news by starting off with something positive. That's the praise that confuses. Especially when you have to dig really deep to find the good things.

It is even worse if you make up excuses for the guy that inadvertently make the problem look like a positive! "You are so good it is only natural that others would be jealous." And then you expect the under-performer to believe that the way he makes people feel is important? Don't laugh. I've seen this happen.

These difficult conversations usually make the boss feel he has done his duty. The under-performer remains as confused as ever. And the problem persists, much to the chagrin of the boss who steeled himself to provide the difficult feedback.

Quit trying to be so nice! Here is a far better approach:

- Identify the factual, specific, observable behavior that is a problem.
- Select a private opportunity to explain those facts.
- Explain the negative impact of that behavior.
- Acknowledge that you don't know 'the other side of the story' or the reasons anyone does what they do, but that something has got to change and you are happy to help figure out what.

This approach is nice too, by the way. But in a different way. This approach is more honest. It is also more respectful because facts are unveiled, judgment isn't. If you stick to the facts and invoke a problem-solving mindset, you can be a respectful partner, not a boss trying not to beat up on an employee.

Don't Throw Your Customer Under the Bus!

I am tickled pink by the incredibly green mileage of my new blue Prius but red with anger over the yellow highlighted 'Excellent' ratings on the sample customer satisfaction survey handed to me by the salesman as I drove off. "If I get less than 90%, Toyota will throw me under the bus," he said.

Toyota wants feedback that the salesman fears and, as a result, the customer suffers. If the salesman does a lousy job, you have three choices:

1. Tell the truth and wonder about the bus and the fate of the salesman.
2. Avoid email and phone calls that ask for feedback.
3. Lie.

That is an ugly choice. Furthermore, it invalidates all the data they are collecting. And I do mean all. I heard the same line when I last bought a Toyota ten years ago. The sickening memory came back to me as soon as I heard it again.

How do you prevent such lunacy?

- When determining any course of action, think about what could go wrong so you can avoid bad decisions and take preventive action.
- Follow up, especially on any action as important as this, to see if it is really working.
- Talk to your customers in multiple ways so you are sure to get the whole story.
- Shop your own shop – anonymously, of course – to get a first hand look at the customer experience.

How Companies Damage Customer Loyalty By Asking For Feedback

I booked a rental car for Budapest using a reputable online service. Several red flags led me to follow up with a phone call. I wasn't sure I could cross international borders. I needed to know more about insurance and when I clicked on the fine print, I was asked in which *state* I was requesting extra insurance. Below the list of choices, I was warned that extra insurance was not available for Texas. What about Hungary, Slovakia, Poland, and the Czech Republic?

The customer service rep was knowledgeable and did her absolute best to find me a rental plan that fit my needs. And, of course, the minute I got off the phone, I received a survey asking about the service I received.

Wait! That's it? All they care about is their customer service rep? They don't care that I just wasted a couple of hours and don't have a car I can drive to Poland because their online sales process is so inadequate?

If I use this survey to express my frustration, which many probably do, a totally helpful employee could lose her job!

Meanwhile, in case you can't tell, the survey has made me madder than the car rental problems.

My recently acquired healthcare service plan deserves to be whacked as well. The insurance company sent a letter explaining how eager they were to be awesome and told me to expect a survey. I was thrilled that they cared. I was glad I'd have the opportunity to tell them about the 10 months I'd spent trying to resolve a billing issue.

But did they ask? No! They wanted to know how many times I visited a doctor and whether I smoked! Despite four pages of questions, they didn't give me a single opportunity to complain about their service! I would have seized any open ended comment field to explain their failings. There wasn't one.

Customer satisfaction surveys are ubiquitous these days. And most are making matters worse, not better.

But this isn't rocket science! To get it right, to gain useful information, and to increase customer loyalty rather than destroy it, you must:

1. Serve the customer, not yourself

A survey that asks for ratings and allows no comments is self-serving. If you care about customers, you need to hear what they have to say.

2. Get out of your silo and examine the full customer experience

A survey that targets one phone call – one tiny sliver of the customer's experience – misses the boat and increases customer frustration. You need to consider the full customer experience from the first to the most recent contact.

3. Be honest about your intentions

A customer satisfaction survey has no business asking about smoking habits unless the customer purchased smoking cessation services. If you want to survey people about their personal habits, don't call it a customer satisfaction survey.

4. Seek information, not statistics

By asking for a simple numeric response to service delivered, you will receive nothing but a report card. While that might help you punish employees or beef up your marketing, it will teach you absolutely nothing that will help you improve.

5. Improve!

When I fill out surveys, it is either because I am thrilled or I want to see improvement. I don't do it because I have nothing better to do with my time! I don't do it because they are fun! I do it because I care. And nothing is more annoying than to discover how little the company cares! Don't ask for people's precious time unless you intend to take action and make real changes to improve their experience.

Monitoring Progress the Wrong Way

Do these questions sound familiar?

- Did you finish X?
- Where do things stand with Y?
- Are we on schedule?
- Are you on budget?
- How long do you think that will take?
- Do you need help?
- What are we going to do about Z?

These are pretty typical questions managers and project managers ask their team members.

Unfortunately, these are dangerous questions. They encourage a check-it-off-the-list, show-progress, and feel-good-mentality. The employee naturally wants to look good and you are generally eager to hear good news so you can turn your attention to more obvious problems. The conversation accomplishes little and you walk away either with a sense of false confidence or a nagging feeling that all is not well.

As manager or project manager, you are rightfully concerned with resources, budgets, and schedules. You want to see a plan and then see progress against that plan. However, plans are only accurate when the task is totally familiar, totally understood, and totally predictable. How often does that occur?

Thus, the most important part of your job is not to monitor the plan. The most important part of your job is to anticipate and prevent problems arising from all the things omitted from the plan, the unfamiliar, the unpredictable, the unknown. And the previous questions do little to uncover those potential problems.

To improve your odds of success and decrease unwelcome surprises, try questions like these:

- What have you learned since we last talked?
- What don't we know yet?
- What are we taking for granted?
- What's changed?
- Why do you think you will finish on time?
- What could go wrong at this point?
- How will we know we've succeeded?
- Whom are we forgetting?

Success requires learning what you don't know as early as possible. Get your whole team focused on anticipating and preventing problems, and you will see your on-time delivery improve while defects and rework drop. This is exactly what happened when I helped the design engineers at Hitachi establish a new design process.

Three Secrets to Success

While I was at dinner recently with a Fortune 500 Executive, we were discussing employee expectations for career advancement. We lamented the ambitious but misguided who don't know what they don't know and feel entitled to success. We bemoaned the techies who are eager to be done but inevitably break something every time they fix something and leave far too many details unfinished. And we shared stories of accomplished individuals who are so nasty, annoying, and/or self-centered no one wants to work with them. In the end, we identified three secrets to success:

1. You've got to get things done.
2. You've got to get them done right.
3. And you can't do it at the expense of others.

Getting things done means taking responsibility, being resourceful and persistent, and finishing on time.

But finishing isn't good enough. You've got to get things done right. Not too well and not half way. You must keep the objectives and constraints in mind, anticipate and prevent problems, and overcome obstacles. Another way to look at this is you have to care. You have to be alert, and you have to think things through. You can not ignore the purpose, process, or people and still get things right.

Last but not least, you can't win at the expense of others, and you can't drive talent away.

If you can get things done right and on time, while also being respectful, helpful, and easy to get along with, you will go far.

Not sure where you stand? Get some feedback from others. Find out how you are perceived. Ask for examples of specific behaviors that exemplify these three characteristics and figure out how you measure up. Not knowing and unrealistic expectations are a bad combination!

Clarity Quiz – Confusing Assumptions with Facts

Which of the following is visible?

1. Attitude.
2. Intelligence.
3. Ambition.
4. Behavior.
5. Skill.

If you selected 'behavior' you are correct!

The vast majority of comments people make about other people are just plain false because they can't know what other people are thinking. Look for facts, don't make assumptions.

In Conclusion – Focus On Observable Behavior And Its Impact

The top secrets for providing useful feedback include:

- Focus on the facts: specific observable behaviors and their impact. Don't make any assumptions or comments about intentions, attitudes, knowledge, motivation, or other invisible personal characteristics.
- Approach problem situations as a partner helping to solve a mutual problem. Acknowledge how little you know about exactly what happened, how, and why. Ask questions. Find out the rest of the story. Offer to help.
- Have the conversation in private as soon as reasonably possible so memories are fresh.
- Don't forget that specific, positive feedback is needed to increase desired behaviors.
- Follow up to acknowledge progress and/or clear up confusion.
- Don't keep employees in positions where they have little chance of succeeding.

Specific, immediate, fact-based feedback makes people less defensive. It puts the focus on a specific set of actions, not on the person. The individual should not be judged or feel judged. Be a partner and a problem solver, not a judge or disciplinarian.

This Could Be Your Competitive Edge, Unless You Delay

"Unclear goals drive activity, not results.
And while activity is epidemic, results rarely are."
Ann Latham

Few truly appreciate the astounding benefits of greater clarity. Those who do are using it to beat the competition. What exactly am I talking about? Greater clarity means:

1. Greater specificity of desired outcomes,
2. Intentionality of process, and,
3. Proper alignment of responsibility.

Every minute of every day.

Clarity allows people to be outcome-focused, action-oriented, and aligned. The benefits are far-ranging:

- Individual and organizational productivity are strong.
- The vast majority of time and energy is dedicated to creating value for which customers are willing to pay.
- Decisions are made by people close to the action without unnecessary approvals and discussion.
- There is less talk and writing but more communication.
- Meetings accomplish twice as much in half the time or less.
- Emails are short, productive, used at the right time, and don't suck up hours of every day.
- Conflict is minimal and healthy debate is plentiful.
- Engagement and commitment are the norm.

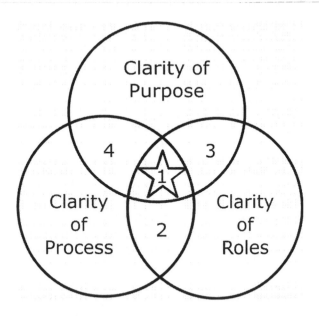

We've looked at the three dimensions essential to achieve *Uncommon Clarity®*: clarity of purpose, process, and roles. Now let's take a look at the overlapping elements on the diagram, see where you need to be and what it looks like when you are missing or weak in an area.

1. *Uncommon Clarity®*

Region #1 on the diagram is where you want to be. In the center of the Venn diagram where clarity of purpose, process, and roles converge.

What does is look like when you are weak in one or more of the three areas?

2. Rube Goldberg machine

Region #2 lacks a clear purpose. If you don't have a clear purpose, you don't really know what you are trying to accomplish. Consequently, you don't make progress!

I'm not talking about your purpose as an organization. I'm talking about what you are trying to accomplish right now. And an hour from now. What does 'done' look like? What identifiable outcome would signify progress? Talk, activity, and effort may feel like progress, but real progress is measured in tangible outcomes. Outcomes such as decisions and plans, as well as more obvious business outcomes such as sales and shipments.

Clarity of purpose increases productivity and improves results. That should seem obvious. What most people don't realize is how little clarity of purpose exists minute to minute and hour to hour. Whether working alone at a desk, in formal meetings, receiving requests from others, or sending emails, there is often little clarity of purpose, little specificity. Just a general sense of the goal. And the farther from the production line, the less clarity there is. A machine operator knows exactly what 'done' looks like. How often can you say the same?

Specifying all outcomes with greater clarity will create tremendous benefits for you and those around you.

3. Earnest Inefficiency

Region #3 is lacking a clear process. If you don't have a clear path, you are wandering. You can't dispute that statement. This is true whether you are sitting alone at your desk or in a meeting. It is true whether you are working on a big project or a small request dropped in your lap this morning. It is especially true when you are working with others. Earnest Inefficiency is characterized by over-doing, under-doing, wandering around, lots of talking, and generally taking a circuitous path to outcomes instead of making clear, discernible progress. You can be sure that machine operator I mentioned is following a clear process. And you can too. You don't have to be making widgets to have a process.

How? If you really understand how to create clarity of purpose, it is easy to create clarity of process.

Why? Because a process is nothing more than a sequence of intermediate outcomes that lead to your desired final outcomes. If you pause before jumping in, establish that sequence, you can straighten the winding path and put an end to wandering.

For common activities, such as decision making, you absolutely should have a clearly understood process to keep everyone on the same page and maximize effectiveness – use *SOAR Through Decisions*™. When creating plans that you need everyone to follow, *DRAW your Plans*, with the simple and effective process. Set *SANITY goals* and use the *SPOT remover* for any problems you encounter.

4. Disempowerment

Region #4 lacks clear roles. Clarity of roles includes assigning responsibilities, but it is so much more. It also requires establishing appropriate sense of ownership and commitment, and ensuring that responsibility is not separated from authority. You want the right people making the right decisions without being dragged down by a hierarchy of approvals and processes. Clarity of roles helps everyone grow, develop self-awareness, take responsibility, and act like true partners. You'll find it's much more important *how* you make decision, than what decisions you make.

As for the remaining regions of the diagram, I hope you are not dwelling in any of them. Specificity creates clarity and clarity creates speed. And that is just the beginning. Embark on a journey to clarity today and you can beat the competition. Making the change to *Uncommon Clarity*® can be a challenge, making the change stick requires changing behavior.

5 Secrets For Making Change Stick

Making change stick is one of my specialties. It would be easier to pop in, teach a few skills, make a few recommendations, and move on. But I'm not satisfied until I believe real results are underway or in sight. What I really enjoy is returning a year or so later to enthusiastic reports from client and staff that they are all still doing as we'd agreed and seeing obvious benefits.

Change fails far more often than not. The reason is that most efforts are comprised of much talk, a couple of decisions, a new rule or two, inevitably some kind of form, and a generous dose of fanfare. None of which guarantee anything actually changes. Change occurs only when people change their behaviors. So let's look at the essential ingredients for making change stick:

1. Desired behaviors must be identified clearly.

Talk is just talk. Action requires action. Change requires sustained action in the form of new on-going behaviors. That won't happen unless people know very specifically what behaviors are desirable. Change occurs when people stop doing some things and start doing other things. Clarity is critical.

2. You, the exemplar, must act like one.

Your staff won't change their behaviors if all they see is business-as-usual coming from you. You must model the desired behaviors every inch of the way. If you don't, don't expect your employees to take you seriously.

3. Those whose behavior must change must be willing to change.

Change by decree is a long, painful slog at best. Usually it fails. If people understand why they need to do things differently and sign up for a new approach willingly, you have a decent shot at success.

4. Practice new behaviors together.

Few hear a new idea and change overnight. Most are usually too busy to even think about how to apply what they've learned, never mind how to integrate it into their daily routine. Overflowing inboxes and old habits present formidable barriers. That is why training is usually a waste of time and money. In order to develop new habits, people need practice, reflection, triggers, and reminders. I don't care if you want to change the way you communicate, run meetings, or develop software. You need to carve out time to practice. If you have a shared and clear understanding of exactly what needs to change, you can work together, remind each other, and consciously practice until you are all well versed in the necessary behaviors.

5. Resist the urge to tweak until you are an expert.

When a new process or method is adopted, there are always snafus. A common reaction is to use every set back, no matter how trivial, as an excuse to tweak the process. Before you know it, you have 'tweaked' yourselves right back to the old routine. It takes a while for a new process to become a standard process. And many people will not fully understand the new process, nor its value, until they get really good at it. Only after you are really good at it should you start messing with it. So, model the desired behaviors and insist others do as well until you can speak from a new place of expertise.

Successful change begins with clarity of purpose, process, and roles. It ends with discipline and practice. When I work with clients, I guide them through this entire sequence until change sticks. This is why they tell me that I always seem as committed to their success as they are. I am, because to stop short just wastes everybody's time. I don't know of any organization that can afford to continue wasteful training and failed change. Embrace these five steps and make your next change stick!

Want More Clarity?

My clients receive *Uncommon Clarity®* in a variety of ways, the most common being:

Clarity-On-Call Advisory Services : For executives who know that immediate strategic clarity allows them to move quickly with greater confidence, smarter decisions, and less risk, but who also know the value of an objective expert who will fearlessly challenge their assumptions and thinking, I provide rapid, behind-the-scenes advice.

Strategic Clarity: Intentional success begins with strategic clarity and alignment. I will lead you to a compelling strategy and strong organizational commitment.

Radical Clarity: *Radical Clarity* is that magic state where objectives and next steps are *always* strategic and crystal clear, *and* in synch with others which makes daily progress easy, fast, and unstoppable. Where employees at all levels create *Clarity-on-the-Fly* to maximize effectiveness, overcome obstacles, and increase profits. This is the answer for leaders who seek a transformational process to expose and resolve the efficiency gap between leadership and production.

Clarity Keynotes: Looking for a provocative and highly interactive talk to awaken your team to the value of *Radical Clarity* and its ability to increase strategic clarity, commitment, productivity, and profits?

Executive Clarity Coaching: Your professional growth will accelerate with strategic clarity – your ability to think strategically; establish direction; create *Clarity-on-the-Fly*; develop employee clarity, self-awareness, and skill; facilitate cognitive processes; and resolve traditional leadership and management shortcomings.

Even More Clarity?

For additional *Uncommon Clarity®* to improve strategic clarity, performance, productivity, and commitment, be sure to investigate the following sources:

Ann's *Clear Thoughts* newsletter

For Ann's award-winning newsletter packed with value, subscribe here: http://bit.ly/clear-thoughts-now

UncommonClarity.com

For hundreds of articles, videos, publications, and podcasts, visit: http://UncommonClarity.com

About Ann Latham

As an expert wilderness canoe guide in areas poorly mapped and fraught with hazards, Ann Latham uses the same laser-like *Uncommon Clarity®* that she brings to her corporate clients. She doesn't want to get lost in the woods and neither do you.

Ann Latham is the founder of Boston area consulting firm *Uncommon Clarity®*, Inc. Her clients represent more than 40 industries and range from for-profit organizations, such as Boeing, Medtronic, and Hitachi, to nonprofit organizations as diverse as Public Television and Smith College.

Ann spent the first half of her career working in high-tech companies, beginning as a software engineer and winding up reporting to the CEO and leading cross-functional and cross-divisional efforts to set strategy and make operational improvements. In 2004, after years of helping only one company at a time, Ann decided to strike out as an independent consultant so she could take her talents to many companies and increase her impact.

Before quitting her job, Ann asked numerous colleagues what it was that she did particularly well that was most uncommon. The responses all pointed to the same thing and she named her company *Uncommon Clarity®* based on those answers.

Upon leaving the corporate world, Ann saved only one of the many framed certificates she had received: "Most Likely to Dispute Recognized Authorities," a good-humored acknowledgement of her constant questioning and challenging of assumptions. She has never looked back.

Ann initially focused on improving client operations, but soon realized that the strategic clarity and alignment essential for success often needed more attention than operations. She quickly changed her business focus to include strategy.

Ann is considered an expert in strategic clarity and the productivity, performance, and commitment that follow.

She's been interviewed and has been written about in 85 media sources, including The New York Times, Bloomberg BusinessWeek, Forbes, Inc., MSNBC.com, and MasterCard.com. She is an expert blogger for Forbes.com. Her business advice also appears in her own global e-newsletter, Clear Thoughts, which won a Constant Contact All-Star Award (for its exceptionally high open rate).

She's an accomplished keynote and workshop speaker, and has spoken to thousands of executives, managers, employees, and MBA students. Of Ann's speaking, famed Ideas Are Free coauthor and Isenberg School of Management professor, Alan G. Robinson says: "Ann Latham is one of the best business speakers I have heard. She is very experienced, the quality of her thinking is extremely high, and she knows how to deliver her message in an entertaining, concise, and convincing way."

In addition to consulting, Ann enjoys travel, sports, and outdoor activities. She has been seen carrying her canoe while riding a unicycle. She took up ice hockey at age 42 when she got tired of watching her daughters have all the fun. (This, she adds, was a seriously humbling experience mostly spent skating toward where the puck used to be.) She's an avid hiker and alpine skier, but also enjoys quieter activities like watching wildlife and curling up with a good book in front of the fire. Her most recent addiction is pickleball, the fastest growing sport in the US.

After visiting 43 countries, 48 US states, and seven Canadian provinces, Ann makes her home in Boston.

She graduated magna cum laude from Tufts University with a degree mathematics.

Testimonials

Ann hit another home run. We wanted to close gaps in roles and responsibilities, reduce confusion, and improve efficiencies and alignment. When my manager's wanted a shift in emphasis, Ann was able to seamlessly adapt her approach as if part of the original plan. We tackled more thorny issues and created more clarity than I ever thought possible. We learned by doing. In some cases, we were able to implement new processes same day. In fact, some supervisors absolutely couldn't wait to get started. I've worked with Ann before. When I need pragmatic changes that will stick, I call Ann. I know I'm going to get what we need. Whatever she would say about herself, I would say she is too modest. She's the best.

Perry Walraven, President and CEO, Performance Controls, Inc.,
a Subsidiary of Hitachi Medical Corporation

Ann's ability to simplify complex issues such that everyone understood their respective roles was a key part of her success. She truly helped us achieve profitable and predictable growth while improving the quality of our methods and processes.

S. W. Emery, Jr., Chairman and CEO, MTS Systems Corporation

I've worked with Ann on three projects at this point, varying from several months to half a day. I'm happy to recommend her because I think so highly of her. I've done a lot of strategic planning, board retreats, and other facilitated activities, and I've never worked with anyone else who comes close to bringing the same value to the table.

Troy Siebels, President & CEO, The Hanover Theatre for the Performing Arts

Ann's style is empathetic, open, and non-judgmental. She somehow seemed to know the room right from the start. She was able to engage everyone, elicit honest feedback, and stimulate creative thinking. This was especially impressive since our group differs significantly in terms of professional expertise and history with the organization. We all felt that our ideas were honored and appreciated. Ann is especially adept at making good choices about further discourse and exposition, pursuing the most fruitful issues and avoiding time wasted on others. She created a productive environment with a level, inviting, and open playing field. I was very pleased with the results.

Jon Abbott, CEO, President & member, WGBH

On a collaborative project with Boeing Phantom Works, Ann did a tremendous job in identifying the cost drivers, producibility issues, and productivity barriers of a supplier organization, all of which were impeding the success of our project. With Ann helping to provide the focus and oversight, the supplier was able to meet their commitments for quality, cost, and schedule.

Ed Gerding, Chief Engineer C-17 St. Louis, The Boeing Company

I had the pleasure of working closely with Ann in my capacity as a volunteer board member of a nonprofit organization. We hired Ann to help the entire board and staff look at our vision and strategy writ large, and grapple with all sorts of complex and challenging questions. She was a tremendous resource, helping to crystallize and focus this extremely broad process, fostering more dialogue and communication between and among all of the participants, and empowering us to consider decisions and the concrete actions needed to move forward. She is sharp, efficient, candid, and has a very effective style and approach that facilitates action and empowers an organization's leaders.

Dave Friedman, Senior Vice President / Special Counsel &
Government Affairs, Boston Red Sox

Ann is an invaluable executive coach. She is a quick, honest, and insightful partner. I have learned as much from her about focused, action-oriented leadership in two months as in a decade of first-hand experience. Ann elevated my awareness of strategy, planning, and execution in ways that immediately impacted my work. I can't recommend Ann more highly.

John Bidwell, Director, Marketing & Digital Strategy, Baystate Health

Ann Latham is one of the best business speakers I have heard. She is very experienced, the quality of her thinking is extremely high, and she knows how to deliver her message in an entertaining, concise, and convincing way.

Dr. Alan G. Robinson, Author: Corporate Creativity: How Innovation & Improvement Actually Happen, *Isenberg School of Management*

Ann showed me a different way to optimize our precious time by focusing on clarity of what is required. She nailed it down to very simple and efficient processes, using clarity, to get things done. A big thumbs up to her way of explaining the only 6 outcomes for a meeting. Thanks for the eye opening session.

*Marco Dufresne, Capital, Engineering and
Operational Excellence lead, Cargill*

'Wow' sums it up nicely. Ann stepped into a delicate, sensitive situation involving a diverse, disjointed group of people with a challenging objective and, in remarkably little time, moved us to a solid, shared conclusion. The way she works is impressive: she has a great handle on people, makes everyone want to work together, ensures every meeting is focused and valuable, and simplifies issues so all understand the challenges and options and can reach shared conclusions. On top of that, I really enjoy working with her.

John Heaps, President, Florence Savings Bank

What I like about working with Ann is how she keeps a group strategically focused while making the process engaging, easy, and humorous. She uncovers common ground, creates opportunity, and guides the group to new shared conclusions in remarkably little time.

Laurie Fenlason, Vice President for Public Affairs, Smith College

Ann Latham transformed our thinking about how our organization works. This discovery led us to a strategic model that solves our pain and opens new opportunities. She truly lives up to her brand of 'uncommon clarity.'

Suzanne Beck, Executive Director,
Greater Northampton Chamber of Commerce

I've never been to a retreat that was so focused, so fast paced, and with such clear progress throughout.

Jay Primack, Managing Partner, Moriarty & Primack P.C.

Ann understood our situation and challenges very quickly. We had five critical issues and she helped us address all five in less time than we thought would be needed for one. She cut to the core, leading us to several important decisions and new ways of working together to be more effective and more strategic. She is fast, refreshingly different, and someone I can recommend highly.

Tim Van Epps, President, The Sandri Companies

Ann is an outstanding team player. Working with a diverse group of manufacturing and design team members, Ann was able to gain consensus for improvement initiatives, win over even the skeptical, and move the team forward toward production-readiness. Every team member has the highest regard for Ann, her professionalism, dedication and energy, and outstanding change management skills.

Dana Badgerow, General Manager, AeroMet Corporation

I called Ann to invite her to meet with our senior team to discuss strategic planning. She asked a few incredibly perceptive questions, declined my invitation, and then gave me free advice over the phone. Her insights and advice were both dead on. She saved us from a costly engagement that would have missed the mark and wasted a lot of time for all of us. If I need her help again, I won't hesitate to call. She proved that she really does practice what she preaches. It is refreshing to find a consultant so clearly looking out for the best interests of her clients.

Mark Pritchard, CFO, Data-Mail Inc.

Ann helps her audiences in a very brief time master such vital skills as improving and speeding decision making in turbulent times, and she does so with wit, energy, and great examples to use as guides.

Alan Weiss, Author: Million Dollar Consulting, *Summit Consulting*

36524292R00152

Made in the USA
Middletown, DE
15 February 2019